CASENO
LEGAL BRIEFS

REMEDIES

**Adaptable to courses utilizing Laycock's
casebook on Modern American Remedies**

NORMAN S. GOLDENBERG, SENIOR EDITOR
PETER TENEN, MANAGING EDITOR

STAFF WRITERS
RICHARD A. LOVICH
KEMP RICHARDSON
RALPH ARMIJO

PUBLISHED BY CASENOTES PUBLISHING CO., INC. 1640 5th ST., SUITE 208 SANTA MONICA, CA 90401

FORMAT FOR THE CASENOTE LEGAL BRIEF

CASE CAPSULE: This boldface section (first three paragraphs) highlights the procedual nature of the case, a short summary of the facts, and the rule of law. This is an invaluable quick-review device designed to refresh the student's memory for classroom discussion and exam preparation.

NATURE OF CASE: This section identifies the form of action (e.g., breach of contract, negligence, battery), the type of proceeding (e.g., demurrer, appeal from trial court's jury instructions) and the relief sought (e.g., damages, injunction, criminal sanctions).

FACT SUMMARY: The fact summary is included to refresh the student's memory. It can be used as a quick reminder of the facts when the student is chosen by an instructor to brief a case.

CONCISE RULE OF LAW: This portion of the brief summarizes the general principle of law that the case illustrates. Like the fact summary, it is included to refresh the student's memory. It may be used for instant recall of the court's holding and for classroom discussion or home review.

FACTS: This section contains all relevant facts of the case, including the contentions of the parties and the lower court holdings. It is written in a logical order to give the student a clear understanding of the case. The plaintiff and defendant are identified by their proper names throughout and are always labeled with a (P) or (D).

ISSUE: The issue is a concise question that brings out the essence of the opinion as it relates to the section of the casebook in which the case appears. Both substantive and procedural issues are included if relevant to the decision.

HOLDING AND DECISION: This section offers a clear and in-depth discussion of the rule of the case and the court's rationale. It is written in easy-to-understand language. When relevant, it includes a thorough discussion of the exceptions listed by the court, the concurring and dissenting opinions, and the names of the judges.

CONCURRENCE / DISSENT: All concurrences and dissents are briefed whenever they are included by the casebook editor.

EDITOR'S ANALYSIS: This last paragraph gives the student a broad understanding of where the case "fits in" with other cases in the section of the book and with the entire course. It is a hornbook-style discussion indicating whether the case is a majority or minority opinion and comparing the principal case with other cases in the casebook. It may also provide analysis from restatements, uniform codes, and law review articles. The editor's analysis will prove to be invaluable to classroom discussion.

CROSS-REFERENCE TO OUTLINE: Wherever possible, following each case is a cross-reference linking the subject matter of the issue to the appropriate place in the *Casenote Law Outline*, which provides further information on the subject.

WINTER v. G.P. PUTNAM'S SONS
938 F.2d 1033 (1991).

NATURE OF CASE: Appeal from summary judgment in a products liability action.

FACT SUMMARY: Winter (P) relied on a book on mushrooms published by Putnam (D) and became critically ill after eating a poisonous mushroom.

CONCISE RULE OF LAW: Strict products liability is not applicable to the expressions contained within a book.

FACTS: Winter (P) purchased The Encyclopedia of Mushrooms, a book published by Putnam (D), to help in collecting and eating wild mushrooms. In 1988, Winter (P), relying on descriptions in the book, ate some wild mushrooms which turned out to be poisonous. Winter (P) became so ill he required a liver transplant. He brought a strict products liability action against Putnam (D), alleging that the book contained erroneous and misleading information that caused his injury. Putnam (D) responded that the information in the book was not a product for purposes of strict products liability, and the trial court granted its motion for summary judgment. The trial court also rejected Winter's (P) actions for negligence and misrepresentation. Winter (P) appealed.

ISSUE: Is strict products liability applicable to the expressions contained within a book?

HOLDING AND DECISION: (Sneed, J.) No. Strict products liability is not applicable to the expressions contained within a book. Products liability is geared toward tangible objects. The expression of ideas is governed by copyright, libel, and misrepresentation laws. The Restatement (Second) of Torts lists examples of the items that are covered by §402A strict liability. All are tangible items, such as tires or automobiles. There is no indication that the doctrine should be expanded beyond this area. Furthermore, there is a strong public interest in the unfettered exchange of ideas. The threat of liability without fault could seriously inhibit persons who wish to share thoughts and ideas with others. Although some courts have held that aeronautical charts are products for purposes of strict liability, these charts are highly technical tools which resemble compasses. The Encyclopedia of Mushrooms, published by Putnam (D), is a book of pure thought and expression and therefore does not constitute a product for purposes of strict liability. Additionally, publishers do not owe a duty to investigate the contents of books that they distribute. Therefore, a negligence action may not be maintained by Winter (P) against Putnam (D). Affirmed.

EDITOR'S ANALYSIS: This decision is in accord with the rulings in most jurisdictions. See Alm v. Nostrand Reinhold Co., Inc., 480 N.E. 2d 1263 (Ill. 1985). The court also stated that since the publisher is not a guarantor of the accuracy of an author's statements, an action for negligent misrepresentation could not be maintained. The elements of negligent misrepresentation are stated in § 311 of the Restatement (Second) of Torts.

[For more information on misrepresentation, see Casenote Law Outline on Torts, Chapter 12, § III, Negligent Misrepresentation.]

NOTE TO STUDENT

OUR GOAL. It is the goal of Casenotes Publishing Company, Inc. to create and distribute the finest, clearest and most accurate legal briefs available. To this end, we are constantly seeking new ideas, comments and constructive criticism. As a user of *Casenote Legal Briefs,* your suggestions will be highly valued. With all correspondence, please include your complete name, address, and telephone number, including area code and zip code.

THE TOTAL STUDY SYSTEM. Casenote Legal Briefs are just one part of the Casenotes TOTAL STUDY SYSTEM. Most briefs are (wherever possible) cross-referenced to the appropriate *Casenote Law Outline,* which will elaborate on the issue at hand. By purchasing a Law Outline together with your Legal Brief, you will have both parts of the Casenotes TOTAL STUDY SYSTEM. (See the advertising in the front of this book for a list of Law Outlines currently available.)

A NOTE ABOUT LANGUAGE. Please note that the language used in *Casenote Legal Briefs* in reference to minority groups and women reflects terminology used within the historical context of the time in which the respective courts wrote the opinions. We at Casenotes Publishing Co., Inc. are well aware of and very sensitive to the desires of all people to be treated with dignity and to be referred to as they prefer. Because such preferences change from time to time, and because the language of the courts reflects the time period in which opinions were written, our case briefs will not necessarily reflect contemporary references. We appreciate your understanding and invite your comments.

A NOTE REGARDING NEW EDITIONS. As of our press date, this Casenote Legal Brief is current and includes briefs of all cases in the current version of the casebook, divided into chapters that correspond to that edition of the casebook. However, occasionally a new edition of the casebook comes out in the interim, and sometimes the casebook author will make changes in the sequence of the cases in the chapters, add or delete cases, or change the chapter titles. Should you be using this Legal Brief in conjuction with a casebook that was issued later than this book, you can receive all of the newer cases, which are available free from us, by sending in the "Supplement Request Form" in this section of the book (please follow all instructions on that form). The Supplement(s) will contain all the missing cases, and will bring your Casenote Legal Brief up to date.

EDITOR'S NOTE. Casenote Legal Briefs are intended to supplement the student's casebook, not replace it. There is no substitute for the student's own mastery of this important learning and study technique. If used properly, *Casenote Legal Briefs* are an effective law study aid that will serve to reinforce the student's understanding of the cases.

SUPPLEMENT REQUEST FORM

At the time this book was printed, a brief was included for every major case in the casebook and for everyy existing supplement to the casebook. However, if a new supplement to the casebook (or a new edition of the casebook) has been published since this publication was printed and if that casebook supplement (or new edition of the casebook) was available for sale at the time you purchased this Casenote Legal Briefs book, we will be pleased to provide you the new cases contained therein AT NO CHARGE when you send us a stamped, self-addressed envelope.

TO OBTAIN YOUR FREE SUPPLEMENT MATERIAL, **YOU MUST FOLLOW THE INSTRUCTIONS BELOW PRECISELY** OR YOUR REQUEST WILL NOT BE ACKNOWLEDGED!

1. Please check if there is in fact an existing supplement and, if so, that the cases are not already included in your Casenote Legal Briefs. Check the main table of cases as well as the supplement table of cases, if any.

2. **REMOVE THIS ENTIRE PAGE FROM THE BOOK.** You MUST send this ORIGINAL page to receive your supplement. This page acts as your proof of purchase and contains the reference number necessary to fill your supplement request properly. No photocopy of this page or written request will be honored or answered. Any request from which the reference number has been removed, altered or obliterated will not be honored.

3. Prepare a STAMPED self-addressed envelope for return mailing. Be sure to use a FULL SIZE (9 X 12) ENVELOPE (MANILA TYPE) so that the supplement will fit and AFFIX ENOUGH POSTAGE TO COVER 3 OZ. **ANY SUPPLEMENT REQUEST NOT ACCOMPANIED BY A STAMPED SELF-ADDRESSED ENVELOPE WILL ABSOLUTELY NOT BE FILLED OR ACKNOWLEDGED.**

4. MULTIPLE SUPPLEMENT REQUESTS: If you are ordering more than one supplement, we suggest that you enclose a stamped, self-addressed envelope for each supplement requested. If you enclose only one envelope for a multiple request, your order may not be filled immediately should any supplement which you requested still be in production. In other words, your order will be held by us until it can be filled completely.

5. Casenotes prints two kinds of supplements. A "New Edition" supplement is issued when a new edition of your casebook is published. A "New Edition" supplement gives you all major cases found in the new edition of the casebook which did not appear in the previous edition. A regular "supplement" is issued when a paperback supplement to your casebook is published. If the box at the lower right is stamped, then the "New Edition" supplement was provided to your bookstore and is *not* available from Casenotes; however, Casenotes will still send you any regular "supplements" which have been printed either before or after the new edition of your casebook appeared and which, according to the reference number at the top of this page, have not been included in this book. If the box is not stamped, Casenotes will send you any supplements, "New Edition" and/or regular, needed to completely update your Casenote Legal Briefs.

NOTE: REQUESTS FOR SUPPLEMENTS WILL NOT BE FILLED UNLESS THESE INSTRUCTIONS ARE COMPLIED WITH!

6. Fill in the following information:

Full title of CASEBOOK ___ **REMEDIES** _____

CASEBOOK author's name **Laycock** _____

Copyright year of new edition or new paperback supplement _____

Name and location of bookstore where this Casenote Legal Brief was purchased _____

Name and location of law school you attend _____

Any comments regarding Casenote Legal Briefs _____

NOTE: IF THIS BOX IS STAMPED, NO NEW EDITION SUPPLEMENT CAN BE OBTAINED BY MAIL.

PUBLISHED BY CASENOTES PUBLISHING CO., INC. 1640 5th ST, SUITE 208 SANTA MONICA, CA 90401

PLEASE PRINT

NAME _____ PHONE _____ DATE _____

ADDRESS/CITY/STATE/ZIP _____

Announcing the First *Totally Integrated* Law Study System

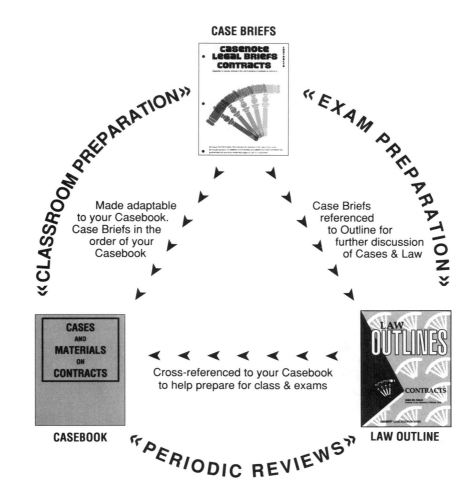

CASE BRIEFS

CASEBOOK

LAW OUTLINE

«CLASSROOM PREPARATION»

«EXAM PREPARATION»

«PERIODIC REVIEWS»

Made adaptable to your Casebook. Case Briefs in the order of your Casebook

Case Briefs referenced to Outline for further discussion of Cases & Law

Cross-referenced to your Casebook to help prepare for class & exams

Casenotes Integrated Study System Makes Studying Easier and More Effective Than Ever!

Casenotes has just made studying easier and more effective than ever before, because we've done the work for you! Through our exclusive integrated study system, most briefs found in this volume of Casenote Legal Briefs are cross-referenced to the corresponding area of law in the Casenote Law Outline series. The cross-reference immediately follows the Editor's Analysis at the end of the brief, and it will direct you to the corresponding chapter and section number in the Casenote Law Outline for further information on the case or the area of law.

This cross-referencing feature will enable you to make the most effective use of your time. While each Casenote Law

Outline focuses on a particular subject area of the law, each legal briefs volume is adapted to a specific casebook. Now, with cross-referencing of Casenote Legal Briefs to Casenote Law Outlines, you can have the best of both worlds – briefs for all major cases in your casebooks and easy-to-find, easy-to-read explanations of the law in our Law Outline series. Casenote Law Outlines are authored exclusively by law professors who are nationally recognized authorities in their field. So using Casenote Law Outlines is like studying with the top law professors.

Try Casenotes new totally integrated study system and see just how easy and effective studying can be.

Casenotes Integrated Study System Does The Work For You!

LAW OUTLINES from CASENOTE™

the Ultimate Outline

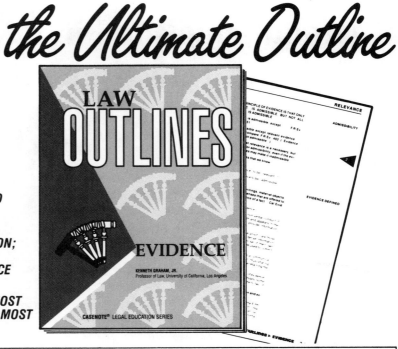

▶ **WRITTEN BY NATIONALLY RECOGNIZED AUTHORITIES IN THEIR FIELD.**

▶ **FEATURING A FLEXIBLE, SUBJECT-ORIENTED APPROACH.**

▶ **CONTAINS: TABLE OF CONTENTS; CAPSULE OUTLINE; FULL OUTLINE; EXAM PREPARATION; GLOSSARY; TABLE OF CASES; TABLE OF AUTHORITIES; CASEBOOK CROSS REFERENCE CHART; INDEX.**

▶ **THE TOTAL LAW SUMMARY UTILIZING THE MOST COMPREHENSIVE STUDY APPROACH IN THE MOST EFFECTIVE, EASY-TO-READ FORMAT.**

REF #	SUBJECT / AUTHORS	RETAIL PRICE
#5260	**ADMINISTRATIVE LAW** by **Charles H. Koch, Jr.,** Dudley W. Woodbridge Professor of Law, College of William and Mary. **Sidney A. Shapiro,** John M. Rounds Professor of Law, University of Kansas. (1996 w/'98 supp.)	(effective 7/1/98) $20.95
#5040	**CIVIL PROCEDURE** by **John B. Oakley,** Professor of Law, University of California, Davis. **Rex R. Perschbacher,** Professor of Law & Associate Dean, Academic Affairs, University of California, Davis. (1996)	$21.95
	COMMERCIAL LAW (*see* 5700 SALES ● 5710 SECURED TRANS. ● 5720 NEG. INSTRUMENTS & PMT. SYST.)	
#5070	**CONFLICT OF LAWS** by **Luther L. McDougal, III,** W.R. Irby Professor of Law, Tulane University. **Robert L. Felix,** James P. Mozingo, III, Prof. of Law, Univ. of S. Carolina. (1996)	$20.95
#5080	**CONSTITUTIONAL LAW** by **Gary Goodpaster,** Prof. of Law, Univ. of California, Davis. (1997 w/'98 supp.)	$23.95
#5010	**CONTRACTS** by **Daniel Wm. Fessler,** Professor of Law, University of California, Davis. (1996)	$20.95
#5050	**CORPORATIONS** AND ALTERNATIVE BUSINESS VEHICLES by **Lewis D. Solomon,** Arthur Selwin Miller Research Prof. of Law, George Washington Univ. **Daniel Wm. Fessler,** Prof. of Law, University of California, Davis. **Arthur E. Wilmarth, Jr.,** Assoc. Prof. of Law, George Washington University. (1997)	$23.95
#5020	**CRIMINAL LAW** by **Joshua Dressler,** Professor of Law, McGeorge School of Law. (1996)	$20.95
#5200	**CRIMINAL PROCEDURE** by **Joshua Dressler,** Prof. of Law, McGeorge School of Law. (1997)	$19.95
#5800	**ESTATE & GIFT TAX** INCLUDING THE FEDERAL GENERATION-SKIPPING TAX by **Joseph M. Dodge,** W.H. Francis Prof. of Law, University of Texas at Austin (w/ supp. due Fall 1998)	$20.95
#5060	**EVIDENCE** by **Kenneth Graham, Jr.,** Professor of Law, University of California, Los Angeles. (1996)	$22.95
#5400	**FEDERAL COURTS** by **Howard P. Fink,** Isadore and Ida Topper Prof. of Law, Ohio State University. **Linda S. Mullenix,** Bernard J. Ward Centennial Prof. of Law, Univ. of Texas. (1997)	$21.95
#5210	**FEDERAL INCOME TAXATION** by **Joseph M. Dodge,** W.H. Francis Professor of Law, University of Texas at Austin (1998).	$21.95
#5300	**LEGAL RESEARCH** by **Nancy L. Schultz,** Associate Professor of Law, Chapman University. **Louis J. Sirico, Jr.,** Professor of Law, Villanova University. (1996)	$20.95
#5720	**NEGOTIABLE INST. & PMT. SYST.** by **Donald B. King,** Professor of Law, Saint Louis University. **Peter Winship,** James Cleo Thompson, Sr. Trustee Prof., SMU. (1995)	$21.95
#5030	**PROPERTY** by **Sheldon F. Kurtz,** Percy Bordwell Professor of Law, University of Iowa. **Patricia Cain,** Professor of Law, University of Iowa (1997)	$21.95
#5700	**SALES** by **Robert E. Scott,** Dean and Lewis F. Powell, Jr. Professor of Law, University of Virginia. **Donald B. King,** Professor of Law, Saint Louis University. (1992)	$20.95
#5710	**SECURED TRANSACTIONS** by **Donald B. King,** Professor of Law, Saint Louis University. (1995 w/'96 supp.)	$19.95
#5000	**TORTS** by **George C. Christie,** James B. Duke Professor of Law, Duke University. **Jerry J. Phillips,** W.P. Toms Professor of Law & Chair, Committee on Admissions, University of Tennessee. (1996 w/'98 supp.)	$21.95
#5220	**WILLS, TRUSTS & ESTATES** by **William M. McGovern,** Professor of Law, University of California, Los Angeles. (1996)	$21.95

rev. 6/1/98

CASENOTE LEGAL BRIEFS

PRICE LIST EFFECTIVE JULY 1, 1998 ● PRICES SUBJECT TO CHANGE WITHOUT NOTICE

Ref. No.	Course	Adaptable to Courses Utilizing	Retail Price
1263	ADMINISTRATIVE LAW	BREYER, STEWART & SUNSTEIN	20.00
1266	ADMINISTRATIVE LAW	CASS, DIVER & BEERMAN	18.00
1260	ADMINISTRATIVE LAW	GELLHORN, B., S., R., S. & F.	18.00
1264	ADMINISTRATIVE LAW	MASHAW, MERRILL & SHANE	19.50
1267	ADMINISTRATIVE LAW	REESE	18.00
1262	ADMINISTRATIVE LAW	SCHWARTZ	19.00
1350	AGENCY & PARTNERSHIP (ENT.ORG)	CONARD, KNAUSS & SIEGEL	22.00
1351	AGENCY & PARTNERSHIP	HYNES	21.00
1690	AMERICAN INDIAN LAW	GETCHES, W. & W.	TBA
1281	ANTITRUST (TRADE REGULATION)	HANDLER, P., G. & W.	18.50
1280	ANTITRUST	AREEDA & KAPLOW	17.50
1283	ANTITRUST	SULLIVAN & HOVENKAMP	19.00
1611	BANKING LAW	MACEY & MILLER	18.00
1303	BANKRUPTCY (DEBTOR-CREDITOR)	EISENBERG	20.00
1305	BANKRUPTCY	JORDAN & WARREN	18.00
1058	BUSINESS ASSOCIATIONS (CORPORATIONS)	KLEIN & RAMSEYER	20.00
1040	CIVIL PROCEDURE	COUND, F., M. & S	21.00
1043	CIVIL PROCEDURE	FIELD, KAPLAN & CLERMONT	21.00
1049	CIVIL PROCEDURE	FREER & PERDUE	17.00
1041	CIVIL PROCEDURE	HAZARD, TAIT & FLETCHER	20.00
1047	CIVIL PROCEDURE	MARCUS, REDISH & SHERMAN	20.00
1044	CIVIL PROCEDURE	ROSENBERG, S. & D.	21.00
1046	CIVIL PROCEDURE	YEAZELL	18.00
1311	COMM'L LAW	FARNSWORTH, H., R., H. & M.	20.00
1312	COMM'L LAW	JORDAN & WARREN	20.00
1310	COMM'L LAW (SALES/SEC.TR./PAY.LAW [Sys.]	SPEIDEL, SUMMERS & WHITE	23.00
1313	COMM'L LAW (SALES/SEC.TR./PAY.LAW)	WHALEY	21.00
1320	COMMUNITY PROPERTY	BIRD	18.50
1630	COMPARATIVE LAW	SCHLESINGER, B., D., H.& W.	17.00
1048	COMPLEX LITIGATION	MARCUS & SHERMAN	18.00
1072	CONFLICTS	BRILMAYER	18.00
1071	CONFLICTS	CRAMTON, C. K., & K.	18.00
1070	CONFLICTS	ROSENBERG, HAY & W.	21.00
1086	CONSTITUTIONAL LAW	BREST & LEVINSON	19.00
1082	CONSTITUTIONAL LAW	COHEN & VARAT	22.00
1088	CONSTITUTIONAL LAW	FARBER, ESKRIDGE & FRICKEY	19.00
1080	CONSTITUTIONAL LAW	GUNTHER & SULLIVAN	21.00
1081	CONSTITUTIONAL LAW	LOCKHART, K., C., S. & F.	19.00
1085	CONSTITUTIONAL LAW	ROTUNDA	21.00
1089	CONSTITUTIONAL LAW (FIRST AMENDMENT)	SHIFFRIN & CHOPER	16.00
1087	CONSTITUTIONAL LAW	STONE, S., S. & T.	20.00
1103	CONTRACTS	BARNETT	22.00
1102	CONTRACTS	BURTON	21.00
1017	CONTRACTS	CALAMARI, PERILLO & BENDER	24.00
1101	CONTRACTS	CRANDALL & WHALEY	21.00
1014	CONTRACTS	DAWSON, HARVEY & H.	20.00
1010	CONTRACTS	FARNSWORTH & YOUNG	19.00
1011	CONTRACTS	FULLER & EISENBERG	22.00
1100	CONTRACTS	HAMILTON, RAU & WEINTRAUB	19.00
1013	CONTRACTS	KESSLER, GILMORE & KRONMAN	24.00
1016	CONTRACTS	KNAPP & CRYSTAL	21.50
1012	CONTRACTS	MURPHY & SPEIDEL	23.00
1018	CONTRACTS	MURRAY	23.00
1015	CONTRACTS	ROSETT	22.00
1019	CONTRACTS	VERNON	21.00
1502	COPYRIGHT	GOLDSTEIN	19.00
1501	COPYRIGHT	NIMMER, M., M. & N.	20.50
1218	CORPORATE TAXATION	LIND, S. L. & R	15.00
1050	CORPORATIONS	CARY & EISENBERG	20.00
1054	CORPORATIONS	CHOPER, COFFEE, & GILSON	22.50
1350	CORPORATIONS (ENTERPRISE ORG.)	CONARD, KNAUSS & SIEGEL	22.00
1053	CORPORATIONS	HAMILTON	20.00
1058	CORPORATIONS (BUSINESS ASSOCIATIONS	KLEIN & RAMSEYER	20.00
1057	CORPORATIONS	O'KELLEY & THOMPSON	19.00
1056	CORPORATIONS	SOLOMON, S., B. & W.	20.00
1052	CORPORATIONS	VAGTS	19.00
1300	CREDITOR'S RIGHTS (DEBTOR-CREDITOR)	RIESENFELD	22.00
1550	CRIMINAL JUSTICE	WEINREB	19.00
1029	CRIMINAL LAW	BONNIE, C., J. & L.	18.00
1020	CRIMINAL LAW	BOYCE & PERKINS	23.00
1028	CRIMINAL LAW	DRESSLER	22.00
1027	CRIMINAL LAW	JOHNSON	21.00
1021	CRIMINAL LAW	KADISH & SCHULHOFER	20.00
1026	CRIMINAL LAW	KAPLAN, WEISBERG & BINDER	19.00
1205	CRIMINAL PROCEDURE	ALLEN, KUHNS & STUNTZ	18.00
1202	CRIMINAL PROCEDURE	HADDAD, Z., S. & B.	21.00
1200	CRIMINAL PROCEDURE	KAMISAR, LAFAVE & ISRAEL	20.00
1204	CRIMINAL PROCEDURE	SALTZBURG & CAPRA	18.00
1203	CRIMINAL PROCEDURE (PROCESS)	WEINREB	19.50
1303	DEBTOR-CREDITOR	EISENBERG	20.00
1300	DEBTOR-CREDITOR (CRED. RTS.)	RIESENFELD	22.00
1304	DEBTOR-CREDITOR	WARREN & WESTBROOK	20.00
1224	DECEDENTS ESTATES (TRUSTS)	RITCHIE, A., & E.(DOBRIS & STERK).	22.00
1222	DECEDENTS ESTATES	SCOLES & HALBACH	22.50
1231	DECEDENTS ESTATES (TRUSTS)	WAGGONER, A. & F.	21.00
	DOMESTIC RELATIONS (see FAMILY LAW)		
3000	EDUCATION LAW (COURSE OUTLINE)	AQUILA & PETZKE	26.50
1670	EMPLOYMENT DISCRIMINATION	FRIEDMAN & STRICKLER	18.00
1671	EMPLOYMENT DISCRIMINATION	ZIMMER, SULLIVAN, R. & C.	19.00
1660	EMPLOYMENT LAW	ROTHSTEIN, KNAPP & LIEBMAN	20.50
1350	ENTERPRISE ORGANIZATION	CONARD, KNAUSS & SIEGEL	22.00
1342	ENVIRONMENTAL LAW	ANDERSON, MANDELKER & T.	17.00
1341	ENVIRONMENTAL LAW	FINDLEY & FARBER	19.00
1345	ENVIRONMENTAL LAW	MENELL & STEWART	18.00
1344	ENVIRONMENTAL LAW	PERCIVAL, MILLER, S. & L.	19.00
1343	ENVIRONMENTAL LAW	PLATER, A., G. & G.	18.00
	EQUITY (see REMEDIES)		

Ref. No.	Course	Adaptable to Courses Utilizing	Retail Price
1217	ESTATE & GIFT TAXATION	BITTKER, CLARK & McCOUCH	16.00
	ETHICS (see PROFESSIONAL RESPONSIBILITY)		
1065	EVIDENCE	GREEN & NESSON	21.00
1066	EVIDENCE	MUELLER & KIRKPATRICK	18.00
1064	EVIDENCE	STRONG, BROUN & M.	23.50
1062	EVIDENCE	SUTTON & WELLBORN	23.00
1061	EVIDENCE	WALTZ & PARK	21.00
1060	EVIDENCE	WEINSTEIN, M., A. & B.	23.50
1244	FAMILY LAW (DOMESTIC RELATIONS)	AREEN	23.00
1242	FAMILY LAW (DOMESTIC RELATIONS)	CLARK & GLOWINSKY	20.00
1245	FAMILY LAW (DOMESTIC RELATIONS)	ELLMAN, KURTZ & BARTLETT	21.00
1246	FAMILY LAW (DOMESTIC RELATIONS)	HARRIS, T. & W.	20.00
1243	FAMILY LAW (DOMESTIC RELATIONS)	KRAUSE, O., E. & G.	25.00
1240	FAMILY LAW (DOMESTIC RELATIONS)	WADLINGTON	21.00
1231	FAMILY PROPERTY LAW (WILLS/TRUSTS)	WAGGONER, A. & F.	21.00
1360	FEDERAL COURTS	FALLON, M. & S. (HART & W.)	20.00
1360	FEDERAL COURTS	HART & WECHSLER (FALLON)	20.00
1363	FEDERAL COURTS	LOW & JEFFRIES	17.00
1361	FEDERAL COURTS	McCORMICK, C. & W.	21.00
1364	FEDERAL COURTS	REDISH & SHERRY	18.00
1089	FIRST AMENDMENT (CONSTITUTIONAL LAW)	SHIFFRIN & CHOPER	16.00
1510	GRATUITOUS TRANSFERS	CLARK, LUSKY & MURPHY	19.00
1650	HEALTH LAW	FURROW, J., J. & S.	18.50
1640	IMMIGRATION LAW	ALEINIKOFF, MARTIN & M.	17.00
1641	IMMIGRATION LAW	LEGOMSKY	20.00
1690	INDIAN LAW (AMERICAN)	GETCHES, W. & W.	TBA
1371	INSURANCE LAW	KEETON	22.00
1372	INSURANCE LAW	YORK, WHELAN & MARTINEZ	20.00
1370	INSURANCE LAW	YOUNG & HOLMES	18.00
1394	INTERNATIONAL BUSINESS TRANSACTIONS	FOLSOM, GORDON & SPANOGLE	16.00
1393	INTERNATIONAL LAW	CARTER & TRIMBLE	17.00
1392	INTERNATIONAL LAW	HENKIN, P., S. & S.	18.00
1390	INTERNATIONAL LAW	OLIVER, F., B., S. & W.	23.00
1331	LABOR LAW	COX, BOK, GORMAN & FINKIN	20.00
1332	LABOR LAW	HARPER & ESTREICHER	21.00
1333	LABOR LAW	LESLIE	19.50
1330	LABOR LAW	MERRIFIELD, S. & C.	20.00
1471	LAND FINANCE (REAL ESTATE TRANS)	BERGER & JOHNSTONE	19.00
1620	LAND FINANCE (REAL ESTATE TRANS)	NELSON & WHITMAN	19.00
1452	LAND USE	CALLIES, FREILICH & ROBERTS	18.00
1421	LEGISLATION	ESKRIDGE & FRICKEY	16.00
1480	MASS MEDIA	FRANKLIN & ANDERSON	16.00
1312	NEGOTIABLE INSTRUMENTS (COMM. LAW)	JORDAN & WARREN	20.00
1541	OIL & GAS	KUNTZ, L., A. & S.	19.00
1540	OIL & GAS	MAXWELL, WILLIAMS, M. & K.	19.00
1560	PATENT LAW	FRANCIS & COLLINS	24.00
1310	PAYMENT LAW [SYST.][COMM. LAW]	SPEIDEL, SUMMERS & WHITE	23.00
1313	PAYMENT LAW (COMM.LAW / NEG. INST.)	WHALEY	23.00
1431	PRODUCTS LIABILITY	OWEN, MONTGOMERY & K.	21.00
1091	PROF. RESPONSIBILITY (ETHICS)	GILLERS	14.00
1093	PROF. RESPONSIBILITY (ETHICS)	HAZARD, KONIAK, & CRAMTON	14.00
1092	PROF. RESPONSIBILITY (ETHICS)	MORGAN & ROTUNDA	14.00
1030	PROPERTY	CASNER & LEACH	22.00
1031	PROPERTY	CRIBBET, J., F. & S.	22.50
1037	PROPERTY	DONAHUE, KAUPER & MARTIN	19.00
1035	PROPERTY	DUKEMINIER & KRIER	19.00
1034	PROPERTY	HAAR & LIEBMAN	21.50
1036	PROPERTY	KURTZ & HOVENKAMP	20.00
1033	PROPERTY	NELSON, STOEBUCK, & W.	21.50
1032	PROPERTY	RABIN & KWALL	21.00
1038	PROPERTY	SINGER	19.50
1621	REAL ESTATE TRANSACTIONS	GOLDSTEIN & KORNGOLD	19.00
1471	REAL ESTATE TRANS. & FIN. (LAND FINANCE)	BERGER & JOHNSTONE	19.00
1620	REAL ESTATE TRANSFER & FINANCE	NELSON & WHITMAN	19.00
1254	REMEDIES (EQUITY)	LAYCOCK	21.00
1253	REMEDIES (EQUITY)	LEAVELL, L., N. & K/F.	22.00
1252	REMEDIES (EQUITY)	RE & RE	24.00
1255	REMEDIES (EQUITY)	SHOBEN & TABB	23.50
1250	REMEDIES (EQUITY)	YORK, BAUMAN & RENDLEMAN	26.00
1310	SALES (COMM. LAW)	SPEIDEL, SUMMERS & WHITE	23.00
1313	SALES (COMM. LAW)	WHALEY	21.00
1312	SECURED TRANS. (COMM. LAW)	JORDAN & WARREN	20.00
1310	SECURED TRANS.	SPEIDEL, SUMMERS & WHITE	23.00
1313	SECURED TRANS. (COMM. LAW)	WHALEY	21.00
1272	SECURITIES REGULATION	COX, HILLMAN, LANGEVOORT	19.00
1270	SECURITIES REGULATION	JENNINGS, M., C. & S.	19.00
1680	SPORTS LAW	WEILER & ROBERTS	18.50
1217	TAXATION (ESTATE & GIFT)	BITTKER, CLARK & McCOUCH	16.00
1219	TAXATION (INDIV. INC.)	BURKE & FRIEL	20.00
1212	TAXATION (FED. INC.)	FREELAND, LIND & STEPHENS	19.00
1211	TAXATION (FED. INC.)	GRAETZ & SCHENK	18.00
1210	TAXATION (FED. INC.)	KLEIN & BANKMAN	19.00
1218	TAXATION (CORPORATE)	LIND, S., L. & R.	15.00
1006	TORTS	DOBBS	20.00
1003	TORTS	EPSTEIN	21.50
1004	TORTS	FRANKLIN & RABIN	18.50
1001	TORTS	HENDERSON, P. & S.	21.50
1000	TORTS	PROSSER, W., S., K. & P.	25.00
1005	TORTS	SHULMAN, JAMES & GRAY	23.00
1281	TRADE REGULATION (ANTITRUST)	HANDLER, P., G. & W.	18.50
1230	TRUSTS	BOGERT, O., H. & H.	21.50
1231	TRUSTS/WILLS (FAMILY PROPERTY LAW)	WAGGONER, A. & F.	21.00
1410	U.C.C.	EPSTEIN, MARTIN, H. & N.	16.00
1223	WILLS, TRUSTS & ESTATES	DUKEMINIER & JOHANSON	20.00
1220	WILLS	MECHEM & ATKINSON	21.00
1231	WILLS/TRUSTS (FAMILY PROPERTY LAW)	WAGGONER, A. & F.	21.00
			(SERIES XLI)

CASENOTES PUBLISHING CO. INC. ● 1640 FIFTH STREET, SUITE 208 ● SANTA MONICA, CA 90401 ● (310) 395-6500

E-Mail Address- casenote@westworld.com
Website-http://www.casenotes.com

PLEASE PURCHASE FROM YOUR LOCAL BOOKSTORE. IF UNAVAILABLE, YOU MAY ORDER DIRECT.*
4TH CLASS POSTAGE (ALLOW TWO WEEKS) $1.00 PER ORDER; 1ST CLASS POSTAGE $3.00 (ONE BOOK), $2.00 EACH (TWO OR MORE BOOKS)
*CALIF. RESIDENTS PLEASE ADD 8¼% SALES TAX

NOTES

HOW TO BRIEF A CASE

A. DECIDE ON A FORMAT AND STICK TO IT

Structure is essential to a good brief. It enables you to arrange systematically the related parts that are scattered throughout most cases, thus making manageable and understandable what might otherwise seem to be an endless and unfathomable sea of information. There are, of course, an unlimited number of formats that can be utilized. However, it is best to find one that suits your needs and stick to it. Consistency breeds both efficiency and the security that when called upon you will know where to look in your brief for the information you are asked to give.

Any format, as long as it presents the essential elements of a case in an organized fashion, can be used. Experience, however, has led *Casenotes* to develop and utilize the following format because of its logical flow and universal applicability.

NATURE OF CASE: This is a brief statement of the legal character and procedural status of the case (e.g., "Appeal of a burglary conviction").

There are many different alternatives open to a litigant dissatisfied with a court ruling. The key to determining which one has been used is to discover *who is asking this court for what*.

This first entry in the brief should be kept as *short as possible*. The student should use the court's terminology if the student understands it. But since jurisdictions vary as to the titles of pleadings, the best entry is the one that apprises the student of who wants what in this proceeding, not the one that sounds most like the court's language.

CONCISE RULE OF LAW: A statement of the general principle of law that the case illustrates (e.g.,"An acceptance that varies any term of the offer is considered a rejection and counteroffer").

Determining the rule of law of a case is a procedure similar to determining the issue of the case. Avoid being fooled by red herrings; there may be a few rules of law mentioned in the case excerpt, but usually only one is *the* rule with which the casebook editor is concerned. The techniques used to locate the issue, described below, may also be utilized to find the rule of law. Generally, your best guide is simply the chapter heading. It is a clue to the point the casebook editor seeks to make and should be kept in mind when reading every case in the respective section.

FACTS: A synopsis of only the essential facts of the case, i.e. those bearing upon or leading up to the issue.

The facts entry should be a short statement of the events and transactions that led one party to initiate legal proceedings against another in the first place. While some cases conveniently state the salient facts at the beginning of the decision, in other instances they will have to be culled from hiding places throughout the text, even from the concurring and dissenting opinions. Some of the "facts" will often be in dispute and should be so noted. Conflicting evidence may be briefly pointed up. "Hard" facts must be included. Both must be *relevant* in order to be listed in the facts entry. It is impossible to tell what is relevant until the entire case is read, as the ultimate determination of the rights and liabilities of the parties may turn on something buried deep in the opinion.

The facts entry should never be longer than one to three *short* sentences.

It is often helpful to identify the role played by a party in a given context. For example, in a construction contract case the identification of a party as the "contractor" or "builder" alleviates the need to tell that that party was the one who was supposed to have built the house.

It is always helpful, and a good general practice, to identify the "plaintiff" and the "defendant." This may seem elementary and uncomplicated, but, especially in view of the creative editing practiced by some casebook editors, it is sometimes a difficult or even impossible task. Bear in mind that the *party presently* seeking something from this court may not be the plaintiff, and that sometimes only the cross-claim of a defendant is treated in the excerpt. Confusing or misaligning the parties can ruin your analysis and understanding of the case.

ISSUE: A statement of the general legal question answered by or illustrated in the case. For clarity, the issue is best put in the form of a question capable of a "yes" or "no" answer. In reality, the issue is simply the Concise Rule of Law put in the form of a question (e.g., "May an offer be accepted by performance?").

The major problem presented in discerning what is *the* issue in the case is that an opinion usually purports to raise and answer several questions. However, except for rare cases, only one such question is really the issue in the case. Collateral issues not necessary to the resolution of the matter in controversy are handled by the court by language known as *"obiter dictum"* or merely *"dictum."* While dicta may be included later in the brief, it has no place under the issue heading.

To find the issue, the student again asks *who wants what* and then goes on to ask *why did that party succeed or fail in getting it.* Once this is determined, the "why" should be turned into a question.

The complexity of the issues in the cases will vary, but in all cases a single-sentence question should sum up the issue. *In a few cases,* there will be two, or even more rarely, three issues of equal importance to the resolution of the case. Each should be expressed in a single-sentence question.

Since many issues are resolved by a court in coming to a final disposition of a case, the casebook editor will reproduce the portion of the opinion containing the issue or issues most relevant to the area of law under scrutiny. A noted law professor gave this advice: "Close the book; look at the title on the cover." Chances are, if it is Property, the student need not concern himself with whether, for example, the federal government's treatment of the plaintiff's land really raises a federal question sufficient to support jurisdiction on this ground in federal court.

The same rule applies to chapter headings designating sub-areas within the subjects. They tip the student off as to what the text is designed to teach. The cases are arranged in a casebook to show a progression or development of the law, so that the preceding cases may also help.

It is also most important to remember to *read the notes and questions* at the end of a case to determine what the editors wanted the student to have gleaned from it.

HOLDING AND DECISION: This section should succinctly explain the rationale of the court in arriving at its decision. In capsulizing the "reasoning" of the court, it should always include an application of the general rule or rules of law to the specific facts of the case. Hidden justifications come to light in this entry; the reasons for the state of the law, the public policies, the biases and prejudices, those considerations that influence the justices' thinking and, ultimately, the outcome of the case. At the end, there should be a short indication of the disposition or procedural resolution of the case (e.g., "Decision of the trial court for Mr. Smith (P) reversed").

The foregoing format is designed to help you "digest" the reams of case material with which you will be faced in your law school career. Once mastered by practice, it will place at your fingertips the information the authors of your casebooks have sought to impart to you in case-by-case illustration and analysis.

B. BE AS ECONOMICAL AS POSSIBLE IN BRIEFING CASES

Once armed with a format that encourages succinctness, it is as important to be economical with regard to the time spent on the actual reading of the case as it is to be economical in the writing of the brief itself. This does not mean "skimming" a case. Rather, it means reading the case with an "eye" trained to recognize into which "section" of your brief a particular passage or line fits and having a system for quickly and precisely marking the case so that the passages fitting any one particular part of the brief can be easily identified and brought together in a concise and accurate manner when the brief is actually written.

It is of no use to simply repeat everything in the opinion of the court; the student should only record enough information to trigger his or her recollection of what the court said. Nevertheless, an accurate statement of the "law of the case," i.e., the legal principle applied to the facts, is absolutely essential to class preparation and to learning the law under the case method.

To that end, it is important to develop a "shorthand" that you can use to make margin notations. These notations will tell you at a glance in which section of the brief you will be placing that particular passage or portion of the opinion.

Some students prefer to underline all the salient portions of the opinion (with a pencil or colored underliner marker), making marginal notations as they go along. Others prefer the color-coded method of underlining, utilizing different colors of markers to underline the salient portions of the case, each separate color being used to represent a different section of the brief. For example, blue underlining could be used for passages relating to the concise rule of law, yellow for those relating to the issue, and green for those relating to the holding and decision, etc. While it has its advocates, the color-coded method can be confusing and time-consuming (all that time spent on changing colored markers). Furthermore, it can interfere with the continuity and concentration many students deem essential to the reading of a case for maximum comprehension. In the end, however, it is a matter of personal preference and style. Just remember, whatever method you use, underlining must be used sparingly or its value is lost.

For those who take the marginal notation route, an efficient and easy method is to go along underlining the key portions of the case and placing in the margin alongside them the following "markers" to indicate where a particular passage or line "belongs" in the brief you will write:

N   (NATURE OF CASE)
CR   (CONCISE RULE OF LAW)
I   (ISSUE)

HC   (HOLDING AND DECISION, relates to the CONCISE RULE
         OF LAW behind the decision)
HR   (HOLDING AND DECISION, gives the RATIONALE or reasoning behind the
decision)
HA   (HOLDING AND DECISION, APPLIES the general principle(s) of law to the
         facts of the case to arrive at the decision)

Remember that a particular passage may well contain information necessary to more than one part of your brief, in which case you simply note that in the margin. If you are using the color-coded underlining method instead of margin notation, simply make asterisks or checks in the margin next to the passage in question in the colors that indicate the additional sections of the brief where it might be utilized.

The economy of utilizing "shorthand" in marking cases for briefing can be maintained in the actual brief writing process itself by utilizing "law student shorthand" within the brief. There are many commonly used words and phrases for which abbreviations can be substituted in your briefs (and in your class notes also). You can develop abbreviations that are personal to you and which will save you a lot of time. A reference list of briefing abbreviations will be found elsewhere in this book.

C. USE BOTH THE BRIEFING PROCESS AND THE BRIEF
AS A LEARNING TOOL

Now that you have a format and the tools for briefing cases efficiently, the most important thing is to make the time spent in briefing profitable to you and to make the most advantageous use of the briefs you create. Of course, the briefs are invaluable for classroom reference when you are called upon to explain or analyze a particular case. However, they are also useful in reviewing for exams. A quick glance at the fact summary should bring the case to mind, and a rereading of the concise rule of law should enable you to go over the underlying legal concept in your mind, how it was applied in that particular case, and how it might apply in other factual settings.

As to the value to be derived from engaging in the briefing process itself, there is an immediate benefit that arises from being forced to sift through the essential facts and reasoning from the court's opinion and to succinctly express them in your own words in your brief. The process ensures that you understand the case and the point that it illustrates, and that means you will be ready to absorb further analysis and information brought forth in class. It also ensures you will have something to say when called upon in class. The briefing process helps develop a mental agility for getting to the *gist* of a case and for identifying, expounding on, and applying the legal concepts and issues found there. Of most immediate concern, that is the mental process on which you must rely in taking law school examinations. Of more lasting concern, it is also the mental process upon which a lawyer relies in serving his clients and in making his living.

GLOSSARY

COMMON LATIN WORDS AND PHRASES ENCOUNTERED IN LAW

A FORTIORI: Because one fact exists or has been proven, therefore a second fact that is related to the first fact must also exist.

A PRIORI: From the cause to the effect. A term of logic used to denote that when one generally accepted truth is shown to be a cause, another particular effect must necessarily follow.

AB INITIO: From the beginning; a condition which has existed throughout, as in a marriage which was void ab initio.

ACTUS REUS: The wrongful act; in criminal law, such action sufficient to trigger criminal liability.

AD VALOREM: According to value; an ad valorem tax is imposed upon an item located within the taxing jurisdiction calculated by the value of such item.

AMICUS CURIAE: Friend of the court. Its most common usage takes the form of an amicus curiae brief, filed by a person who is not a party to an action but is nonetheless allowed to offer an argument supporting his legal interests.

ARGUENDO: In arguing. A statement, possibly hypothetical, made for the purpose of argument, is one made arguendo.

BILL QUIA TIMET: A bill to quiet title (establish ownership) to real property.

BONA FIDE: True, honest, or genuine. May refer to a person's legal position based on good faith or lacking notice of fraud (such as a bona fide purchaser for value) or to the authenticity of a particular document (such as a bona fide last will and testament).

CAUSA MORTIS: With approaching death in mind. A gift causa mortis is a gift given by a party who feels certain that death is imminent.

CAVEAT EMPTOR: Let the buyer beware. This maxim is reflected in the rule of law that a buyer purchases at his own risk because it is his responsibility to examine, judge, test, and otherwise inspect what he is buying.

CERTIORARI: A writ of review. Petitions for review of a case by the United States Supreme Court are most often done by means of a writ of certiorari.

CONTRA: On the other hand. Opposite. Contrary to.

CORAM NOBIS: Before us; writs of error directed to the court that originally rendered the judgment.

CORAM VOBIS: Before you; writs of error directed by an appellate court to a lower court to correct a factual error.

CORPUS DELICTI: The body of the crime; the requisite elements of a crime amounting to objective proof that a crime has been committed.

CUM TESTAMENTO ANNEXO, ADMINISTRATOR (ADMINISTRATOR C.T.A.): With will annexed; an administrator c.t.a. settles an estate pursuant to a will in which he is not appointed.

DE BONIS NON, ADMINISTRATOR (ADMINISTRATOR D.B.N.): Of goods not administered; an administrator d.b.n. settles a partially settled estate.

DE FACTO: In fact; in reality; actually. Existing in fact but not officially approved or engendered.

DE JURE: By right; lawful. Describes a condition that is legitimate "as a matter of law," in contrast to the term "de facto," which connotes something existing in fact but not legally sanctioned or authorized. For example, de facto segregation refers to segregation brought about by housing patterns, etc., whereas de jure segregation refers to segregation created by law.

DE MINIMUS: Of minimal importance; insignificant; a trifle; not worth bothering about.

DE NOVO: Anew; a second time; afresh. A trial de novo is a new trial held at the appellate level as if the case originated there and the trial at a lower level had not taken place.

DICTA: Generally used as an abbreviated form of obiter dicta, a term describing those portions of a judicial opinion incidental or not necessary to resolution of the specific question before the court. Such nonessential statements and remarks are not considered to be binding precedent.

DUCES TECUM: Refers to a particular type of writ or subpoena requesting a party or organization to produce certain documents in their possession.

EN BANC: Full bench. Where a court sits with all justices present rather than the usual quorum.

EX PARTE: For one side or one party only. An ex parte proceeding is one undertaken for the benefit of only one party, without notice to, or an appearance by, an adverse party.

EX POST FACTO: After the fact. An ex post facto law is a law that retroactively changes the consequences of a prior act.

EX REL.: Abbreviated form of the term ex relatione, meaning, upon relation or information. When the state brings an action in which it has no interest against an individual at the instigation of one who has a private interest in the matter.

FORUM NON CONVENIENS: Inconvenient forum. Although a court may have jurisdiction over the case, the action should be tried in a more conveniently located court, one to which parties and witnesses may more easily travel, for example.

GUARDIAN AD LITEM: A guardian of an infant as to litigation, appointed to represent the infant and pursue his/her rights.

HABEAS CORPUS: You have the body. The modern writ of habeas corpus is a writ directing that a person (body) being detained (such as a prisoner) be brought before the court so that the legality of his detention can be judicially ascertained.

IN CAMERA: In private, in chambers. When a hearing is held before a judge in his chambers or when all spectators are excluded from the courtroom.

IN FORMA PAUPERIS: In the manner of a pauper. A party who proceeds in forma pauperis because of his poverty is one who is allowed to bring suit without liability for costs.

INFRA: Below, under. A word referring the reader to a later part of a book. (The opposite of supra.)

IN LOCO PARENTIS: In the place of a parent.

IN PARI DELICTO: Equally wrong; a court of equity will not grant requested relief to an applicant who is in pari delicto, or as much at fault in the transactions giving rise to the controversy as is the opponent of the applicant.

IN PARI MATERIA: On like subject matter or upon the same matter. Statutes relating to the same person or things are said to be in pari materia. It is a general rule of statutory construction that such statutes should be construed together, i.e., looked at as if they together constituted one law.

IN PERSONAM: Against the person. Jurisdiction over the person of an individual.

IN RE: In the matter of. Used to designate a proceeding involving an estate or other property.

IN REM: A term that signifies an action against the res, or thing. An action in rem is basically one that is taken directly against property, as distinguished from an action in personam, i.e., against the person.

INTER ALIA: Among other things. Used to show that the whole of a statement, pleading, list, statute, etc., has not been set forth in its entirety.

INTER PARTES: Between the parties. May refer to contracts, conveyances or other transactions having legal significance.

INTER VIVOS: Between the living. An inter vivos gift is a gift made by a living grantor, as distinguished from bequests contained in a will, which pass upon the death of the testator.

IPSO FACTO: By the mere fact itself.

JUS: Law or the entire body of law.

LEX LOCI: The law of the place; the notion that the rights of parties to a legal proceeding are governed by the law of the place where those rights arose.

MALUM IN SE: Evil or wrong in and of itself; inherently wrong. This term describes an act that is wrong by its very nature, as opposed to one which would not be wrong but for the fact that there is a specific legal prohibition against it (malum prohibitum).

MALUM PROHIBITUM: Wrong because prohibited, but not inherently evil. Used to describe something that is wrong because it is expressly forbidden by law but that is not in and of itself evil, e.g., speeding.

MANDAMUS: We command. A writ directing an official to take a certain action.

MENS REA: A guilty mind; a criminal intent. A term used to signify the mental state that accompanies a crime or other prohibited act. Some crimes require only a general mens rea (general intent to do the prohibited act), but others, like assault with intent to murder, require the existence of a specific mens rea.

MODUS OPERANDI: Method of operating; generally refers to the manner or style of a criminal in committing crimes, admissible in appropriate cases as evidence of the identity of a defendant.

NEXUS: A connection to.

NISI PRIUS: A court of first impression. A nisi prius court is one where issues of fact are tried before a judge or jury.

N.O.V. (NON OBSTANTE VEREDICTO): Notwithstanding the verdict. A judgment n.o.v. is a judgment given in favor of one party despite the fact that a verdict was returned in favor of the other party, the justification being that the verdict either had no reasonable support in fact or was contrary to law.

NUNC PRO TUNC: Now for then. This phrase refers to actions that may be taken and will then have full retroactive effect.

PENDENTE LITE: Pending the suit; pending litigation underway.

PER CAPITA: By head; beneficiaries of an estate, if they take in equal shares, take per capita.

PER CURIAM: By the court; signifies an opinion ostensibly written "by the whole court" and with no identified author.

PER SE: By itself, in itself; inherently.

PER STIRPES: By representation. Used primarily in the law of wills to describe the method of distribution where a person, generally because of death, is unable to take that which is left to him by the will of another, and therefore his heirs divide such property between them rather than take under the will individually.

PRIMA FACIE: On its face, at first sight. A prima facie case is one that is sufficient on its face, meaning that the evidence supporting it is adequate to establish the case until contradicted or overcome by other evidence.

PRO TANTO: For so much; as far as it goes. Often used in eminent domain cases when a property owner receives partial payment for his land without prejudice to his right to bring suit for the full amount he claims his land to be worth.

QUANTUM MERUIT: As much as he deserves. Refers to recovery based on the doctrine of unjust enrichment in those cases in which a party has rendered valuable services or furnished materials that were accepted and enjoyed by another under circumstances that would reasonably notify the recipient that the rendering party expected to be paid. In essence, the law implies a contract to pay the reasonable value of the services or materials furnished.

QUASI: Almost like; as if; nearly. This term is essentially used to signify that one subject or thing is almost analogous to another but that material differences between them do exist. For example, a quasi-criminal proceeding is one that is not strictly criminal but shares enough of the same characteristics to require some of the same safeguards (e.g., procedural due process must be followed in a parol hearing).

QUID PRO QUO: Something for something. In contract law, the consideration, something of value, passed between the parties to render the contract binding.

RES GESTAE: Things done; in evidence law, this principle justifies the admission of a statement that would otherwise be hearsay when it is made so closely to the event in question as to be said to be a part of it, or with such spontaneity as not to have the possibility of falsehood.

RES IPSA LOQUITUR: The thing speaks for itself. This doctrine gives rise to a rebuttable presumption of negligence when the instrumentality causing the injury was within the exclusive control of the defendant, and the injury was one that does not normally occur unless a person has been negligent.

RES JUDICATA: A matter adjudged. Doctrine which provides that once a court of competent jurisdiction has rendered a final judgment or decree on the merits, that judgment or decree is conclusive upon the parties to the case and prevents them from engaging in any other litigation on the points and issues determined therein.

RESPONDEAT SUPERIOR: Let the master reply. This doctrine holds the master liable for the wrongful acts of his servant (or the principal for his agent) in those cases in which the servant (or agent) was acting within the scope of his authority at the time of the injury.

STARE DECISIS: To stand by or adhere to that which has been decided. The common law doctrine of stare decisis attempts to give security and certainty to the law by following the policy that once a principle of law as applicable to a certain set of facts has been set forth in a decision, it forms a precedent which will subsequently be followed, even though a different decision might be made were it the first time the question had arisen. Of course, stare decisis is not an inviolable principle and is departed from in instances where there is good cause (e.g., considerations of public policy led the Supreme Court to disregard prior decisions sanctioning segregation).

SUPRA: Above. A word referring a reader to an earlier part of a book.

ULTRA VIRES: Beyond the power. This phrase is most commonly used to refer to actions taken by a corporation that are beyond the power or legal authority of the corporation.

ADDENDUM OF FRENCH DERIVATIVES

IN PAIS: Not pursuant to legal proceedings.

CHATTEL: Tangible personal property.

CY PRES: Doctrine permitting courts to apply trust funds to purposes not expressed in the trust but necessary to carry out the settlor's intent.

PER AUTRE VIE: For another's life; in property law, an estate may be granted that will terminate upon the death of someone other than the grantee.

PROFIT A PRENDRE: A license to remove minerals or other produce from land.

VOIR DIRE: Process of questioning jurors as to their predispositions about the case or parties to a proceeding in order to identify those jurors displaying bias or prejudice.

NOTES

TABLE OF CASES

A

American Broadcasting Companies v. Wolf 47
American National Bank & Trust Co.v. Weyerhaeuser
    Co. 67

Ariola v. Nigro 43

B

Bailey v. Proctor 31
Baker v. F & F Investment Co. 92
Beagle v. Vasold 20
Bigelow v. RKO Radio Pictures 18
Bivens v. Six Unknown Named Agents of Federal Bureau of
    Narcotics 96
Brook v. James A. Cullimore & Co. 39
Brunswick Corp. v. Pueblo Bowl-O-Mat 19
Buck v. Morrow 9
Burlington, City of v. Dague 84

C

Campbell Soup Co. v. Wentz 40
Campbell Soup Co. v. Wentz 89
Cardinal Chemical Co. v. Morton International 53
Carey v. Piphus 24
Carroll v. President of Princess Anne 49
Catena v. Seidl 75
Cavnar v. Quality Control Parking 26
Chatlos Systems v. National Cash Register 8
Chauffeurs Local No. 391 v. Terry 102
Coyne-Delany Co. v. Capital Development Board 48
Credit Bureau of Broken Bow v. Moninger 78

D

Decatur County AG-Services v. Young 7
Dixie National Bank v. Chase 79
Doran v. Salem Inn 55

E

Edelman v. Jordan 50
Eisen v. Carlisle & Jacquelin 104
Erie Trust Co., In re 64
Etheridge v. Medical Center Hospitals 21
Evans v. Jeff D. 86
Evra Corp. v. Swiss Bank Corp. 17

F

Farash v. Sykes Datatronics, Inc. 62
Farmers Export Co. v. M/V Georgis Prois 13
Fifty Acres of Land, United States v. 5

G

Georgia-Pacific Co, United States v. 90
General Building Contractors Association v.
    Pennsylvania 36
Griffin v. County School Board 75
Grimshaw v. Ford Motor Co. 70

H

Hall, United States v. 77
Hand v. Dayton-Hudson 56
Harlow v. Fitzgerald 100
Hathahley, United States v. 4
Helfend v. Southern California Rapid Transit District 15
Hicks v. Clayton 62
Hills v. Gautreaux 35
Humble Oil & Refining Co. v. Harang 28
Hutto v. Finney 32

I

International Union, United Mine Workers v.
    Clinchfield Coal Co. 74

J

Jones and Laughlin Steel Corp. v. Pfeifer 26

K

Kearney & Trecker Corp. v. Master Engraving Co. 12
Knaysi v. A.H. Robins Co. 94

L

Lakeshore Hills v. Adcox 48
Levka v. City of Chicago 23
Linda R.S. v. Richard D. 97
Los Angeles Memorial Coliseum Commission v. National
    Football League 47

M

Maier Brewing Co. v. Fleischmann Distilling Corp. 59
Marriage of Logston, In re 80
Marshall v. Goodyear Tire & Rubber Co. 28
Mazzocone v. Willing 46
Meinrath v. Singer Co. 10
Merrill Lynch, Pierce, Fenner & Smith v. Curran 97
Milliken v. Bradley 32
Missouri v. Jenkins 33
Mutual Benefit Life Insurance Co. v. JMR Electronics
    Corp. 61

N

NAACP v. NAACP Legal Defense & Educational Fund 91

Continued on next page

NOTES

TABLE OF CASES (Continued)

Nashville, Chattanooga & St. Louis Railway v. Wallace 52
Neri v. Retail Marine Corp. 7
Newman Machine Co. v. Newman 55
New York, City of v. Citisource, Inc. 81
Nicholson v. Connecticut Halfway House, Inc. 29
Norfolk and Western Railway v. Liepelt 25
North American Coin & Currency, In re 63
Northern Delaware Industrial Development Corp. v. E.W.
    Bliss Co. 14
Northern Delaware Industrial Development Corp. v. E.W.
    Bliss Co. 44

O
Olwell v. Nye & Nissen Co. 58
O'Brien v. Eli Lilly & Co. 93

P
Pardee v. Camden Lumber Co. 39
Pinter v. Dahl 88
Pruitt v. Allied Chemical Corp. 16

R
Riss v. City of New York 99
Riverside, City of v. Rivera 83
Robinson v. Robinson 66
Rogers v. Rogers 65
Rufo v. Inmates of the Suffolk County Jail 34

S
S.J. Groves & Sons Co. v. Warner Co. 15
Sampson v. Murray 49
Sheldon v. Metro-Goldwyn Pictures Corp. 60
Smith v. Department of Insurance 22
Smith v. Bolles 9
Snepp v. United States 59
Southwestern Bell Telephone Co. v. Norwood 18
Southwestern Bell Telephone Co. v. Norwood 30
Steffel v. Thompson 54
Stump v. Sparkman 101
Swann v. Charlotte-Mecklenburg Board of
    Education 31
Swedish Hospital Corp. v. Shalala 85

T
Texaco, Inc. v. Pennzoil Co. 11
Thompson v. Commonwealth 41
Thompson v. Commonwealth 54
Transcontinental Gas Pipe Line Corp. v. American
    Nat'l Petroleum Co. 72

Trinity Church v. John Hancock Mutual Life
    Insurance Co. 6
TXO Production Corp. v. Alliance Resources
    Corp. 71

U
United States Fidelity & Guaranty Co. v. Bimco Iron &
    Metal Corp. 90
USM Corp. v. Marson Fastener Corp. 60

V
Van Wagner Advertising Corp. v. S & M
    Enterprises 42

W
W.E. Erickson Construction v. Congress-Kenilworth
    Corp. 82
W.T. Grant Co., United States v. 29
Walker v. City of Birmingham 76
Welch v. Kosasky 68
Willing v. Mazzocone 45
Winston Research Corp. v. Minnesota Mining &
    Manufacturing Co. 30
Women's Equity Action League v. Cavazos 98

CHAPTER 2*
PAYING FOR HARM: COMPENSATORY DAMAGES

QUICK REFERENCE RULES OF LAW

Tort

1. **The Basic Principle: Restoring Plaintiff to His Rightful Position.** An award of damages based on the commission of a tort must be based on the principle that the injured party must be restored to the same position he was in had the tort not been committed. (United States v. Hatahley)

Property = Market VALUE

2. **Value as the Measure of the Rightful Position.** Just compensation under the Fifth Amendment must be measured by the market value of the property unless the market value is too difficult to determine. (United States v. Fifty Acres of Land)

Damage to property = diminution in value, if too difficult cost of replacement/

3. **Value as the Measure of the Rightful Position.** Reasonable costs of reconstruction or replacement are *reconstruction* allowed as a measure of damages where the diminution of market value of property cannot be determined. *(reasonable)* (Trinity Church v. John Hancock Mutual Life Insurance Co.)

Damage to crops = difference in value before/after injury at time of harvest

4. **Value as the Measure of the Rightful Position.** The measure of damages for partial destruction of a growing crop is the difference in the crop's value immediately before and after the injury, with value determined at the time of harvest. (Decatur County Ag-Services v. Young)

Seller of goods = reliance + expectancy: lost profits + incidental damages.

5. **Reliance and Expectancy as Measures of the Rightful Position.** Under the U.C.C., the seller of goods rejected by a breaching buyer may recover his lost profits and incidental damages caused by the breach. (Neri v. Retail Marine Corp.) *(Breaching buyer)*

Breach of Warranty

6. **Reliance and Expectancy as Measures of the Rightful Position.** For breach of warranty, the correct measure of damages is the difference between the fair market value of the goods accepted and the value they would have had if they had been as warranted. (Chatlos Systems v. National Cash Register Corp.)

Fraud - Sale of Stock

7. **Reliance and Expectancy as Measures of the Rightful Position.** The proper measure of damages for fraud in the sale of stock is the actual loss suffered due to the deception, not the purported value of the stock. (Smith v. Bolles)

Breach of lease of property

8. **Consequential Damages.** A party may recover any consequential damages reasonably anticipated by the parties for the breach of a lease of real property. (Buck v. Morrow)

money debt = interest only

9. **Consequential Damages.** A creditor may recover only interest on late payment of money due and no consequential damages are recoverable. (Meinrath v. Singer Co.)

Tortious interference w/ Contractual relations

10. **Consequential Damages.** The plaintiff in an action for tortious interference with an existing contract is entitled to recover the full pecuniary loss of the benefit it would have been entitled to under the contract, as well as consequential and punitive damages. (Texaco v. Pennzoil Co.)

Consequential Damages DISCLAIMER

11. **The Parties' Power to Specify the Remedy.** A consequential damages disclaimer is not invalidated by the failure of a limited remedy provision unless it is unconscionable. (Kearney & Trecker Corp. v. Master Engraving Co.)

Liquidated damages clause.

12. **The Parties' Power to Specify the Remedy.** Liquidated damages provisions are allowable where they are a reasonable forecast of the anticipated actual damages. (Farmers Export Co. v. M/V Georgis Prois)

*There are no cases in Chapter 1.

6th floor center for law + financial markets. overlook.

Specific Performance in Construction K

13. **The Parties' Power to Specify the Remedy.** Absent special circumstances or a compelling public interest, a court of equity should not order the specific performance of any construction contract in a situation in which it would be impractical to carry out such an order. (Northern Illinois Gas Co. v. Energy Cooperative)

Buyer's duty to mitigate damages

14. **Avoidable Consequences, Offsetting Benefits, and Collateral Sources.** A buyer may choose any one of several available methods of mitigating damages to recover consequential damages for the seller's breach. (S.J. Groves & Sons Co. v. Warner Co.)

Collateral Source Rule

15. **Avoidable Consequences, Offsetting Benefits, and Collateral Sources.** The collateral source rule prohibits the introduction of evidence of compensation paid to the plaintiff by a source completely independent from the tortfeasor to partially or fully compensate for the injuries sustained. (Helfend v. Southern California Rapid Transit District)

D's negligence + proximate cause

16. **Proximate Cause and Related Problems.** Recovery may be obtained for damages proximately caused by the defendant's negligence. (Pruitt v. Allied Chemical Corp.)

D's negligence avoidable by plaintiff

17. **Proximate Cause and Related Problems.** A party may not recover consequential damages when such were consequences of the defendant's negligence which were avoidable by the plaintiff. (Evra Corp. v. Swiss Bank Corp.)

Special Damages

18. **Proximate Cause and Related Problems.** A telephone company is not liable for special damages for failure to furnish connection to a person if it had no notice of the circumstances out of which the damages might arise. (Southwestern Bell Telephone Co. v. Norwood)

Damages should be sufficiently certain to be recoverable.

19. **The Certainty Requirement.** A jury may make a just and reasonable estimate of damages based on the evidence presented, and its award need not be based on precise mathematical computations. (Bigelow v. RKO Radio Pictures)

remedial goals to further policy

20. **Substantive Policy Goals.** Antitrust relief is not available in every case in which a large corporation takes over smaller businesses and causes readjustments in the market share of other participants. (Brunswick Corp. v. Pueblo Bowl-O-Mat)

In some states AttNy can argue Per Diem bas

21. **Personal Injuries and Death.** ~~Statutory limitations on the amount of recovery for medical malpractice are~~ ~~constitutional.~~ (Beagle v. Vasold)   *for pain + suffering*

med - MAL caps

22. **Personal Injuries and Death.** Statutory limitations on the amount of recovery for medical malpractice are constitutional. (Etheridge v. Medical Center Hospitals)

caps on P.I. damages

23. **Personal Injuries and Death.** A statutory limitation on damages for noneconomic losses violates the Florida Constitution. (Smith v. Department of Insurance)

24. **Dignitary and Constitutional Harms.** A court may exercise its discretion in reducing a jury verdict when the evidence indicated the verdict is grossly excessive. (Levka v. City of Chicago)

25. **Dignitary and Constitutional Harms.** Absent proof of actual injury caused by a denial of procedural due process, only nominal damages may be awarded. (Carey v. Piphus)

non- flexibility of jury awards.

26. **Taxes, Time, and the Value of Money.** It Is error for a trial judge to refuse to admit evidence of the nontaxability of jury awards or to instruct the jury thereof. (Norfolk & Western Railway v. Liepelt)

27. **Taxes, Time, and the Value of Money.** Prejudgment interest may be awarded to a prevailing plaintiff in a personal injury action on damages that have accrued by the time of judgment. (Cavnar v. Quality Control Parking)

28. **Taxes, Time, and the Value of Money.** Federal courts may choose the manner in which to discount the present value of future earnings and are not bound by a rule of state law. (Jones & Laughlin Steel Corp. v. Pfeifer)

UNITED STATES v. HATHAHLEY
257 F.2d 920 (10th Cir. 1958).

NATURE OF CASE: Appeal from award of damages for trespass.

NOTES:

FACT SUMMARY: The Government (D) appealed from the district court's calculation of damages for trespass to Hathahley's (P) and other plaintiffs' property.

CONCISE RULE OF LAW: An award of damages based on the commission of a tort must be based on the principle that the injured party must be restored to the same position he was in had the tort not been committed.

FACTS: The Government (D) tortiously rounded up and sold farm animals owned by Hathahley (P) and other Indians. The district court determined a set amount of damages for each animal and multiplied that amount by the number of animals lost by each plaintiff. It also arrived at a sum for mental distress and awarded each plaintiff an equal amount. The Government (D) appealed, contending the award was arbitrary and not based on substantial evidence.

ISSUE: Are tort damages based on the principle that the injured party should be placed in the position he would have been in had the tort not been committed?

HOLDING AND DECISION: (Pickett, J.) Yes. Tort damages are based upon the principle that the injured party be placed in the same position he would have been in had the tort not occurred. By making a blanket damage determination, the court failed to consider the damages actually incurred by each plaintiff. Each had different levels of economic damage incurred as each had differently valued animals. Also each suffered a different level of mental distress. Reversed and remanded.

EDITOR'S ANALYSIS: This case illustrates the fundamental remedial goal in tort law. Placing a person in the position he would have been in without the tort is often speculative and always inexact. This is especially true where the damages are based on lost profits or mental distress.

UNITED STATES v. FIFTY ACRES OF LAND
469 U.S. 24 (1984).

NATURE OF CASE: Appeal from judgment in action for just compensation for public condemnation.

FACT SUMMARY: The United States (D) condemned property used as a landfill by the city of Duncanville (P), which contended that it was entitled to be compensated the amount that it would have to pay to obtain a substitute facility.

CONCISE RULE OF LAW: Just compensation under the Fifth Amendment must be measured by the market value of the property unless the market value is too difficult to determine.

FACTS: In 1978, as part of a flood control project in Texas, the United States (D) condemned a fifty-acre lot owned by the city of Duncanville (P). The property had been used since 1969 as a landfill by Duncanville (P). In order to replace the landfill, Duncanville (P) bought a larger site and developed a better facility which cost $723,624. Duncanville (P) brought an action for just compensation for the condemnation against the United States (D). The trial court awarded Duncanville (P) $225,000 as the fair market value of the condemned fifty-acre lot. The court of appeals reversed and remanded, holding that Duncanville (P) was entitled to the amount reasonably spent to create a functionally equivalent landfill facility. The United States (D) appealed.

ISSUE: Should compensation under the Fifth Amendment be measured by the market value of the property?

HOLDING AND DECISION: (Stevens, J.) Yes. Just compensation under the Fifth Amendment must be measured by the market value of the property unless the market value is too difficult to determine. The long established rule of the Court is that just compensation is measured by the market value of the property at the time of the taking. Deviation from this measure of compensation has only been required when the market value is too difficult to ascertain or when its application would result in manifest injustice. The fair market value is not ascertainable only when a property, such as a road, is seldom, if ever, sold in the open market. Otherwise, the market measure of compensation achieves a fair balance between the public's need and the claimant's loss. The obligation to replace a condemned facility does not justify a departure from the general rule. The adoption of a substitute-facilities doctrine, whereby the measure of damages would be the cost of replacing the condemned property, would add uncertainty and complexity to the valuation proceeding and would add subjective values to the process. The fair-market-value measure is the most objective standard and is better suited to most cases. In this case, there is a robust market for landfill properties, and the fair market value of the fifty acres owned by Duncanville (P) was readily determinable by the trial court through expert testimony. There has been no showing of manifest injustice. Therefore, the fair market value of the property was the appropriate measure of damages. Reversed.

CONCURRENCE: (O'Connor) When a local government is obligated to obtain a substitute facility in order to provide an essential service, and the market value deviates significantly from the amount necessary to make the locality whole, the market value measure is inappropriate under the Just Compensation Clause.

EDITOR'S ANALYSIS: Value measure of damages is usually proved by price quotations in the open market for similar properties. Also, experts typically estimate the fair market value of property. The Duncanville (P) property presented a problem because the fifty acres was valued for its function as a landfill, and the value of the property didn't necessarily correspond to the value of the function.

NOTES:

TRINITY CHURCH v. JOHN HANCOCK
MUTUAL LIFE INSURANCE CO.
502 N.E.2d 532 (Mass. 1987).

NATURE OF CASE: Appeal of an award of damages for injury to property.

FACT SUMMARY: Trinity Church's (P) building was damaged during the construction of the nearby John Hancock (D) building, and it sought damages for the structural harm to the church.

CONCISE RULE OF LAW: Reasonable costs of reconstruction or replacement are allowed as a measure of damages where the diminution of market value of property cannot be determined.

FACTS: Trinity Church (P) was built in 1876 in Boston. It was constructed almost entirely of stone masonry, which cracks over time and cannot be repaired except by reconstruction. By 1968, the church had experienced settlement of four inches, but because the subsidence was fairly uniform, no structural stress or damage had resulted. During construction of the John Hancock (D) Tower Building next to Trinity Church (P) between 1968 and 1972, the foundation of the church was undermined by a failure of the excavation system at the Hancock (D) site. Trinity's (P) foundation settled unevenly and produced cracks that affected the structural integrity of the church. Trinity (P) sought compensation for the structural damages and quantified the damages based upon the percentage change in the structure in terms of the church's ultimate "takedown" condition, the point at which reconstruction would be necessary. The jury awarded Trinity (P) $3.6 million for the structural damage, and John Hancock (D) appealed.

ISSUE: Are reasonable costs of reconstruction or replacement allowed as a measure of damages where the diminution of market value of property cannot be determined?

HOLDING AND DECISION: (Lynch, J.) Yes. Reasonable costs of reconstruction or replacement are allowed as a measure of damages where the diminution of market value of property cannot be determined. The general rule for measuring property damage is diminution in market value but is not a universal test because it does not always afford a correct measure of indemnity. Special purpose properties, such as properties owned by religious organizations, are not subject to the general rule because there is no active market from which the market value may be determined. For special purpose properties, other proofs of value may be used, such as the cost of reproduction, less depreciation, or the cost of restoration or replacement. These costs must meet a test of reasonableness, and the restoration must be necessary in light of the damage inflicted. In certain situations, restoration might be uneconomical and improper if the expenses are disproportionate to the injury. Here, Trinity's (P) method of computing structural damages was reasonable because it computed the percentage of damage caused by Hancock (D) against the ultimate necessity of reconstructing the church. Thus, where sections of the church would require reconstruction at a certain point and Hancock (D) caused damages representing 50% of the total, Trinity (P) was awarded half of the total restoration costs. This is appropriate even though Trinity (P) does not yet have to restore the church because the remedy reasonably reflects the depreciation caused by Hancock (D). Affirmed.

DISSENT: (O'Connor, J.) Damages are only appropriate as compensation for actual losses. Here, there is no evidence that Trinity (P) has suffered any present loss of use or enjoyment of the church or diminution of its market value. The estimated future restoration costs are simply too speculative.

EDITOR'S ANALYSIS: Buildings such as churches pose special problems in these cases because there is truly no market value. There are virtually no other uses for a large church building. Courts generally rule that the value to an owner should exclude sentimental considerations, although it is not clear whether the religious significance of a church should be considered where it must be rebuilt.

NOTES:

DECATUR COUNTY AG-SERVICES v. YOUNG
426 N.E.2d 644 (Ind. 1981).

NATURE OF CASE: Appeal from award of damages.

FACT SUMMARY: Decatur (D) contended the amount of damages awarded to Young (P) for damages to his crops was speculative and not based on sufficient evidence.

CONCISE RULE OF LAW: The measure of damages for partial destruction of a growing crop is the difference in the crop's value immediately before and after the injury, with value determined at the time of harvest.

FACTS: Young's (P) soybean crop was partially destroyed by Decatur's (D) negligent pesticide spraying. Young (P) sued and was awarded damages based upon a determination of the size of the crop had it not been partially destroyed, and the price per unit obtained through the sale of the remaining beans after the next year's planting season. Decatur (D) appealed the computation of damages, contending such was speculative and should have been based on the value of the beans at the time of harvest.

ISSUE: Is the measure of damages for lost or injured crops based on the market value at the time of harvest?

HOLDING AND DECISION: (Prentice, J.) Yes. The measure of damages for the loss or injury to growing crops is the difference between the crop's value immediately before and after the injury or partial destruction. Value must be determined at the first point where the crops have a marketable quality which is at the time of harvest. The fact that Young (P) successfully speculated that the price of beans would increase does not allow the basis of damages to shift to the point of sale. Therefore, the damage award was improper. Reversed and remanded.

EDITOR'S ANALYSIS: The court in this case went on to indicate that the damage award had to take into consideration the decreased expenses caused by the partial destruction of the crops. However, because in this case the record indicated that Young (P) did his own harvesting, storage, and transportation of the crop, no such incidental savings were realized.

NERI v. RETAIL MARINE CORP.
30 N.Y.2d 393, 285 N.E.2d 311 (1972).

NATURE OF CASE: Appeal from award of damages for lost profits.

FACT SUMMARY: Neri (P) contended Retail Marine (D) could not recover lost profits and incidental damages for Neri's (P) failure to purchase a boat he had contracted to buy.

CONCISE RULE OF LAW: Under the U.C.C., the seller of goods rejected by a breaching buyer may recover his lost profits and incidental damages caused by the breach.

FACTS: Neri (P) ordered a boat from Retail Marine (D) and tendered a deposit of $4,250. After delivery, Retail Marine (D) received a letter from Neri's (P) attorney indicating Neri (P) could not go through with the purchase and demanding return of the deposit. Retail Marine (D) refused and after several months resold the boat for the same price Neri (P) agreed to pay. Neri (P) sued to recover his deposit, and Retail Marine (D) cross-complained for lost profits, contending it would have sold two boats in the absence of Neri's (P) breach. It also sued for consequential damages in the form of storage costs incurred due to the delay in sale. Liability against Neri (P) was established by summary judgment, and the issue of damages was certified for appeal.

ISSUE: May an aggrieved seller recover lost profits and incidental damages for a buyer's breach?

HOLDING AND DECISION: (Gibson, J.) Yes. Under the U.C.C., a seller of goods rejected by a breaching buyer may recover lost profits and incidental damages. Had Neri (P) not breached, Retail Marine (D) clearly would have realized two boat sales instead of one, and, therefore, it is entitled to recover the lost profits as damages. Further, the storage costs were incidentally incurred due to the breach. Neri (P) is entitled to return of his deposit, subject to an offset for the recoverable damages.

EDITOR'S ANALYSIS: This case illustrates a court protecting a nonbreaching party's expectancy interest in granting relief from breach. A party is granted not only out-of-pocket damages, but what he expected to realize on the contract, placing him in the position he would have been in had the contract not been breached.
NOTES:

CHATLOS SYSTEMS v. NATIONAL CASH REGISTER
670 F.2d 1304 (3d Cir. 1982).

NATURE OF CASE: Appeal from an award of damages for breach of warranty.

FACT SUMMARY: Chatlos Systems, Inc. (P) contended the computer system it purchased from National Cash Register (D) did not function as warranted.

CONCISE RULE OF LAW: For breach of warranty, the correct measure of damages is the difference between the fair market value of the goods accepted and the value they would have had if they had been as warranted.

FACTS: After negotiating for several months, Chatlos (P) purchased an NCR model 399/656 computer from NCR (D) for $46,020. The computer system was warranted to have certain specified capabilities, which it failed to perform. Using a "benefit of the bargain" formula, the district court determined the damages to be $201,826.50. NCR (D) contended the contract price for the system was the only competent record evidence of the value of the system as warranted. However, the district court relied on the testimony of Chatlos' (P) expert witness, who estimated the value of a computer system that would perform all of the functions that the purchased system had been warranted to perform to be in the $100,000 to $150,000 range. This appeal followed.

ISSUE: For breach of warranty, is the difference between the fair market value of the goods accepted and the value they would have had if they had been as warranted the correct measure of damages?

HOLDING AND DECISION: (Aldisert, J.) Yes. For breach of warranty, the correct measure of damages is the difference between the fair market value of the goods accepted and the value they would have had if they had been as warranted. (N.J.S.A. § 12A:2-714(2)). Contract price is not necessarily the same as market value. Chatlos (P) did not order merely a specific computer model, but an NCR (D) computer system with specified capabilities. The computer purchased, the NCR 399/656, would not perform the functions warranted. The trial court, confronted with conflicting value estimates submitted by the parties, made a credibility determination on the factual findings. That determination may be reversed only if the court's factual determinations were clearly erroneous. They were not so. Affirmed.

DISSENT: (Rosenn, C.J.) No probative evidence supports the award of damages for the breach of warranty in a sum amounting to almost five times the purchase price of the goods. The measure of damages has been misapplied. The focus of the statute is upon the goods accepted — not other hypothetical goods which may perform equivalent functions. The purpose of the statute is to put the buyer in the same position he would have been in if there had been no breach. The remedies for breach of warranty were intended to compensate the buyer for his loss, not to give him a windfall or treasure trove.

EDITOR'S ANALYSIS: The dissent's point is that Chatlos (P) was not an unsophisticated purchaser. Further, they had bargained with NCR (D) for several months before deciding on the system eventually purchased. In other words, they bargained for a cheap system, and that is what they got. However, it appears NCR's (D) company officials knew in advance the system which they warranted and which was ordered by Chatlos (P) would not deliver the program bargained for and the program that was warranted.

NOTES:

SMITH v. BOLLES
132 U.S. 125 (1889).

NATURE OF CASE: Appeal from award of damages for fraud.

FACT SUMMARY: Bolles (P) was awarded damages based on the value of stock as it would have been had Smith's (D) fraudulent representations been true.

CONCISE RULE OF LAW: The proper measure of damages for fraud in the sale of stock is the actual loss suffered due to the deception, not the purported value of the stock.

FACTS: Smith (D) fraudulently represented stock to have great value and sold it to Bolles (P) for $6,000. Bolles (P) sued for fraud and was awarded damages in an amount equal to what the stock would have been worth if the representations had been true. Smith (D) appealed, contending this was an improper measure of damages.

ISSUE: Is the proper measure of damages for the fraudulent sale of stock the actual loss to the defrauded buyer?

HOLDING AND DECISION: (Fuller, C.J.) Yes. The proper measure of damages for fraud in the sale of stock is the actual loss suffered due to the deception, not the purported value of the stock as represented. The action here was not brought for breach of contract, thus no expectancy interest was lost. Bolles (P) was defrauded in the amount of the price paid for the stock, and this was the correct measure of damages. Reversed.

EDITOR'S ANALYSIS: The key distinction in this case is the contrast between the remedial theories of tort and contract actions. Many commentators have criticized the unavailability of expectancy damages in tort, especially where the same set of facts could be used as the basis of a cause of action for tort or contract.

BUCK v. MORROW
2 Tex. Civ. App. 361, 21 S.W. 398 (1893).

NATURE OF CASE: Appeal from denial of damages for breach of lease.

FACT SUMMARY: The trial court held Buck (P) could not recover consequential damages for Morrow's (D) breach of lease.

CONCISE RULE OF LAW: A party may recover any consequential damages reasonably anticipated by the parties for the breach of a lease of real property.

FACTS: Morrow (D) leased pasture land to Buck (P) for the latter's cattle. The lease included a clause requiring Morrow (D) to compensate Buck (P) for any damages which resulted from any sale of the land. Morrow (D) subsequently sold the land, and Buck (P) was dispossessed. He lost several head of cattle, was required to hire extra help to watch the cattle, and incurred other expenses in an attempt to find alternative pasture land. Buck (P) sued, praying for damages not only for the lost value of the lease, but for the consequential damages incurred. The trial court held no consequential damages were recoverable, and Buck (P) appealed.

ISSUE: Are consequential damages recoverable for the breach of a lease?

HOLDING AND DECISION: (Stephens, J.) Yes. Consequential damages are recoverable for breach of lease. Such damages directly result from the breach and should be fully recoverable. Therefore, the trial court erred in refusing such an award. Reversed.

EDITOR'S ANALYSIS: Traditionally the only damages recoverable for the breach of a lease were based upon the difference between the rent to be paid and the actual value of the unexpired lease term. Consequential damages are generally recognized; however, there are some areas, such as eminent domain, where they continue to be denied.

MEINRATH v. SINGER CO.
87 F.R.D. 422 (S.D.N.Y. 1980).

NATURE OF CASE: Action for damages for nonpayment of sums due under contract.

FACT SUMMARY: Meinrath (P) sought consequential damages for Singer's (D) failure to make timely bonus payments under a written agreement.

CONCISE RULE OF LAW: A creditor may recover only interest on late payment of money due and no consequential damages are recoverable.

FACTS: Meinrath (P) entered into a contract with Singer (D) which required the latter to pay him bonus compensation under certain circumstances. Meinrath (P) sued, contending Singer's (D) failure to make timely payments of such bonuses caused his other business ventures to fail. He contended such failures were consequential damages recoverable for Singer's (D) actions as Singer (D) knew of the dependency of such ventures on the timely payments. Singer (D) moved for summary judgment, contending consequential damages were not recoverable.

ISSUE: May a creditor recover consequential damages for the debtor's failure to timely pay sums owed?

HOLDING AND DECISION: (Weinfeld, J.) No. A creditor may not recover consequential damages for the debtor's failure to timely pay sums owed. The only type of damages available are interest payments at the legal limit. This case presents no agreement to pay consequential damages, and thus none are recoverable. Motion for summary judgment granted.

EDITOR'S ANALYSIS: This case follows the holding in Loudon v. Taxing District, 104 U.S. 771 (1881). That case handed down the rule recognizing interest as the proper type of damages for failure to pay a money debt. This is true whether or not the consequential damages were well known by the debtor.

NOTES:

TEXACO, INC. v. PENNZOIL CO.

Tex. Ct. of Civ. App., 729 S.W.2d 768 (1987).

NATURE OF CASE: Appeal from award of compensatory and punitive damages for tortious interference with contractual relations.

FACT SUMMARY: Pennzoil's (D) "agreement in principle" to acquire three-sevenths of the stock of Getty Oil was breached when Texaco (P) made a higher bid for, and announced its plans to merge with, Getty.

CONCISE RULE OF LAW: The plaintiff in an action for tortious interference with an existing contract is entitled to recover the full pecuniary loss of the benefit it would have been entitled to under the contract, as well as consequential and punitive damages.

FACTS: Pennzoil (D) agreed "in principle" to buy three-sevenths of the stock of Getty Oil. Although the deal was structured as a purchase of stock, Pennzoil (D) principally was attempting to secure for itself the 1.008 billion barrels of oil which constituted Getty's proven reserves. However, Texaco (P) outbid Pennzoil (D) and announced its plans to merge with Getty. Pennzoil (D) sued Texaco (P) in tort for intentional interference with contractual relations. At trial Pennzoil (D) presented expert testimony that its cost to find reserves equivalent to those it had bought from Getty for $3.40/barrel was $10.87/barrel. Thus, Pennzoil's (D) "replacement cost" for the Getty reserves was $7.53 billion, which the jury awarded Pennzoil (D) as compensatory damages. The jury also awarded Pennzoil (D) $3 billion in punitive damages. Texaco (P) appealed, arguing that Pennzoil's (D) damages were more accurately calculated as the difference between the market value of the Getty stock and its contract price at the time of breach, and that the punitive damage award was excessive.

ISSUE: Is the plaintiff in an action for tortious interference with contractual relations entitled to recover the full pecuniary loss of the benefits it would have been entitled to under the contract, in addition to consequential and punitive damages?

HOLDING AND DECISION: (Warren, J.) Yes. The plaintiff in an action for tortious interference with contractual relations is entitled to recover the full pecuniary loss of the benefits it would have been entitled to under the contract, plus consequential and punitive damages. Here Pennzoil (D) proved through expert testimony that the "replacement cost" of the reserves it would have obtained under its contract to buy Getty equalled $7.53 billion, the figure awarded by the jury. The jury acted reasonably in arriving at this award, even if Pennzoil's (D) obligation to the Getty shareholders might have required it to restructure or reorganize Getty rather than take Getty reserves in kind, and even if some of the Getty reserves consisted of low-grade heavy crude rather than the more valuable light crude Pennzoil (D) eventually bought to replace the

Getty reserves. Nor was Pennzoil (D) required to use a post-tax figure in its loss calculations, given the unavailability of incentives for exploration and development when the taxpayer only acquires reserves, because it did figure in as an offset its $1 billion recapture tax liability. Finally, Pennzoil (D) was not required to prove its damages to a certainty; uncertainty is tolerated when difficulty in calculating damages is attributable to the defendant's conduct. However, the $3 billion punitive damage award against Texaco (P), which represented about 40% of the compensatory damage award, was excessive, and the trial court abused its discretion in not suggesting a remittitur. Although a punitive damage award should punish and deter, it should not, as here, confiscate or overstate its purpose. The punitive damage award will be reduced to $1 billion. Affirmed, as modified.

EDITOR'S ANALYSIS: The "replacement cost" model for compensatory damages here was not the only one the jury was allowed to consider or upon which it could have based its award. Pennzoil (D) also introduced expert testimony on equally viable models, such as discounted cash flow (reducing to present value the income Pennzoil (D) would have received from its acquisition of Getty), and the cost of acquiring a "related" business. It might also be noted that plaintiffs can even recover damages for tortious interference with contracts that are legally unenforceable. See, e.g., Harris v. Perl, 41 N.J. 455, 197 A.2d 359 (1964) ("no matter what flaws a lawyer can find" interference with contract is "a wrong").

NOTES:

**KEARNEY & TRECKER CORP. v.
MASTER ENGRAVING CO.**
527 A.2d 429 (N.J. 1987).

NATURE OF CASE: Appeal of an award of damages for breach of warranty.

FACT SUMMARY: Master Engraving (P) bought a machine tool from Kearney (D) which did not operate properly and sought consequential damages for lost profits.

CONCISE RULE OF LAW: A consequential damages disclaimer is not invalidated by the failure of a limited remedy provision unless it is unconscionable.

FACTS: Master Engraving (P), a manufacturer of component parts for industrial application, bought a computer-controlled machine tool from Kearney (D) in 1978. The purchase price was $167,000, and the sales proposal from Kearney (D) included a warranty provision which stated that consequential damages were disclaimed and that Master's (P) remedy was limited to repair or replacement. The machine tool malfunctioned frequently and was inoperable from 25% to 50% of the time in the first year. Master (P) brought suit for breach of warranty and introduced evidence regarding lost profits due to the breach. The trial court instructed the jury that it could award consequential damages if it found that Kearney's (D) limited remedy provision had failed its essential purpose. The jury awarded $57,000 to Master (P), and Kearney (D) appealed.

ISSUE: Is a consequential damages disclaimer invalidated by the failure of a limited remedy provision?

HOLDING AND DECISION: (Stein, J.) No. A consequential damages disclaimer is not invalidated by the failure of a limited remedy provision unless it is unconscionable. Under the Uniform Commercial Code, consequential damages are recoverable if the seller breaches. However, § 2-719(3) provides that consequential damages may be limited or excluded unless it is unconscionable. Still, at least minimum adequate remedies must be available to the buyer. Section 2-719(2) states that where a seller's limited remedy fails of its essential purpose, all remedies provided for in the Code are available. Limited remedies provisions are typically repair or replacement clauses included by the seller to allow for the opportunity to make the goods conforming and limiting the risks of consequential damages. Where a limited warranty contains an express disclaimer of consequential damages but the remedy fails of its essential purpose, courts are split on whether the disclaimer is still valid. Some courts have ruled that since there is an integral relationship between the exclusion and the limited remedy, the failure of the repair or replacement provision should invalidate the disclaimer. Other courts have concluded that the exclusion of consequential damages should be viewed independently. This is the better rule because sellers' immunity from liability for consequential damages is indispensable in routine transactions. Also, the buyer is protected by other remedies in the Code and also when the disclaimer is unconscionable. Although Kearney (D) was unable to repair or replace the machine tool sold to Master (P) so that is was operable during the first year, the exclusion of consequential damages contained in the sales agreement is not invalidated. Furthermore, Master (P) has an adequate remedy if it brings suit for breach of the limited warranty. Therefore, the award of damages must be reversed, and the case is remanded.

EDITOR'S ANALYSIS: As the decision noted, there is significant split of authority on this issue. One court has staked out a middle position which holds that the disclaimer does not survive if the breach is fundamental and total. See RRX Industries v. Lab-Con, 772 F.2d 543 (9th Cir. 1985). In a sales contract, the seller can either limit its warranty obligations or its liability for breach of the warranty. Only disclaimers of warranties must be conspicuous.

NOTES:

FARMERS EXPORT CO. v. M/V GEORGIS PROIS
799 F.2d 159 (5th Cir. 1986).

NATURE OF CASE: Appeal from the enforcement of a liquidated damages provision.

FACT SUMMARY: Farmers Export (P), a grain elevator, applied a liquidated damages provision when Marfo (D), a shipowner, remained docked at berth after being requested to leave.

CONCISE RULE OF LAW: Liquidated damages provisions are allowable where they are a reasonable forecast of the anticipated actual damages.

FACTS: Marfo (D), a shipowner, docked at Farmers Export (P), a grain elevator, and then was unable to leave because of striking crew members. Under the terms of the docking agreement, ships were charged $5,000 an hour for the time that they remained docked after being requested to leave. This liquidated damages provision was intended to help regulate the activities of the grain elevator and to serve as an estimate of the average cost to Farmers (P) if vessel loading was interrupted. Farmers (P) billed Marfo (D) $5,000 an hour for the twenty-eight hours that the ship remained docked after Farmers (P) requested that it leave. Marfo (D) responded that the liquidated damages clause should be struck down as a penalty. The trial court enforced the provision, and Marfo (D) appealed.

ISSUE: Are liquidated damages provisions allowable where they are a reasonable forecast of the anticipated actual damages?

HOLDING AND DECISION: (Garwood, J.) Yes. Liquidated damages provisions are allowable where they are a reasonable forecast of the anticipated actual damages. Liquidated damages provisions will be disallowed if they are punitive in nature. The only proper purpose of damages is to place the nonbreaching party in the position it would have been in without the breach. A two-part test is used to determine whether a stipulated damage clause is a penalty. The first factor is the anticipated or actual loss caused by the breach. The fixed amount is reasonable if it approximates the actual loss resulting from a particular breach. The second factor is the difficulty of proof of loss. Liquidated damages are given more leeway where it is relatively difficult to prove the damages resulting from the breach. Farmers (P) proved that it was difficult to prove the damages resulting from failure to leave the dock. Damages depend on the capacity of specific ships waiting to dock and weather conditions. Therefore, since damages in this case are difficult to prove, a court should be more lenient in determining whether the amount fixed by Farmers (P) is a reasonable approximation. Although one purpose of the provision was to encourage shipowners to vacate the dock when ordered, which is not a valid reason for liquidated damages, the evidence indicates that $5,000 an hour was a reasonable forecast of the anticipated damages to Farmers (P) for the failure of a ship to leave the dock. This was proved in part by testimony that the actual damages in the present case approximated $5,000 an hour. Therefore, the liquidated damages provision imposed by Farmers (P) on Marfo (D) was not a penalty. Affirmed.

EDITOR'S ANALYSIS: This decision applies the same test for liquidated damages as the Restatement (Second) of Contracts, § 356. The Restatement also provides that if the actual damages in a given case are simple to prove, the difficulty in predicting the damages at the time of the contract is irrelevant. Thus, the liquidated damages provision will be disregarded.

NOTES:

NORTHERN DELAWARE INDUSTRIAL DEVELOPMENT CORP. v. E.W. BLISS CO.
245 A.2d 432 (Del. Ch. 1968).

NATURE OF CASE: Motion for order to compel requisitioning of laborers.

FACT SUMMARY: Northern Delaware (NDIDC) (P) sought an order for equitable relief requesting that E.W. Bliss (D), the firm that contracted to remodernize a steel fabricating plant, hire a second shift of workers so the remodernization would be speeded up.

CONCISE RULE OF LAW: Absent special circumstances or a compelling public interest, a court of equity should not order the specific performance of any construction contract in a situation in which it would be impractical to carry out such an order.

FACTS: NDIDC (P) and E.W. Bliss (D) contracted for the remodernization of a steel fabricating plant owned by Phoenix Steel Corp. (P). A proposal made by E.W. Bliss' (D) prime subcontractor contained a "Working Schedule" provision that contemplated a double shift work schedule when one of the steel mills had to be shut down to carry out the remodernization. Work on the massive project did not proceed as rapidly as originally contemplated, and E.W. Bliss (D) was clearly behind schedule. NDIDC (P) and Phoenix Steel (P) made a motion for equitable relief requesting in essence that, as contemplated in the "Working Schedule," E. W. Bliss (D) be required to hire sufficient laborers to form a night shift during the period that one of the steel mills was shut down in an effort to speed up work on the project. The court noted that there was some question as to the availability of laborers to grant the relief sought.

ISSUE: Absent special circumstances or a compelling public interest, should a court of equity order specific performance of any construction contract in a situation in which it would be impractical to carry out such an order?

HOLDING AND DECISION: (Marvel, V.C.) No. Absent special circumstances or a compelling public interest, a court of equity should not order the specific performance of any construction contract in a situation in which it would be impractical to carry out such an order. In the present situation, the parties have contracted for a massive, complex remodernization, and the contract is nowhere near finished. There is some question as to the availability of laborers to grant the relief requested. There is no question that a court of equity has jurisdiction to grant the relief sought, but in light of the imprecision of the contractual provision being relied on, and the impracticability, if not impossibility, of enforcing the order, specific performance of the provision contemplating the second shift would be inappropriate. NDIDC (P) and Phoenix Steel (P) will be able to sue later for damages resulting from actionable building delays.

EDITOR'S ANALYSIS: While the court's fears in ending up supervising the enforcement of the order may have been premature, they certainly were not groundless. In a situation where the parties are cooperative, supervision might be practically nonexistent. If, however, the parties are noncooperative, the court would, in a situation like the present case, be forced to become involved in every minute detail of the remodernization.

NOTES:

S.J. GROVES & SONS CO. v. WARNER CO.
576 F.2d 524 (3d Cir. 1978).

NATURE OF CASE: Appeal from award of damages for breach of contract.

FACT SUMMARY: The trial court held as a matter of law that Groves (P) should have obtained concrete elsewhere, and its failure to do so precluded recovery of consequential damages.

CONCISE RULE OF LAW: A buyer may choose any one of several available methods of mitigating damages to recover consequential damages for the seller's breach.

FACTS: Warner (D) contracted with Groves (P) to supply concrete according to Groves' instructions. Warner (D) consistently failed to make timely deliveries and the general contractor threatened to stop payment for services. Groves (P) continued to use Warner (D) even though another concrete company was available. Groves (P) subsequently sued and was awarded damages; however, consequential damages were denied on the basis Groves (P) failed to mitigate damages by employing the other concrete company. Groves (P) appealed.

ISSUE: May a buyer of goods choose any one of several reasonable methods of mitigating damages in order to recover consequential damages caused by the seller's breach?

HOLDING AND DECISION: (Weis, J.) Yes. A buyer may choose any one of several available methods of mitigating damages to recover consequential damages for the seller's breach. Groves (P) was not bound to drop Warner (D) in favor of another seller as the change may have incurred greater damages than those sustained with Warner (D). Therefore, Groves (P) cannot be penalized for choosing an available means of mitigation-staying with the breaching seller based upon assurances of satisfactory performance. Thus, consequential damages should have been awarded. Reversed.

EDITOR'S ANALYSIS: The court in this case discussed and rejected the applicability of the avoidable consequences doctrine. This doctrine holds a defendant harmless where the plaintiff could have avoided the consequences through affirmative action. The doctrine is analogous to contributory or comparative negligence theories.

HELFEND v. SOUTHERN CALIFORNIA RAPID TRANSIT DISTRICT
2 Cal. 3d 1, 465 P.2d 61 (1970).

NATURE OF CASE: Appeal from award of damages for personal injury.

FACT SUMMARY: The Southern California Rapid Transit District (RTD) (D) contended it could introduce evidence of insurance benefits received by Helfend (P) to reduce the recoverable damages.

CONCISE RULE OF LAW: The collateral source rule prohibits the introduction of evidence of compensation paid to the plaintiff by a source completely independent from the tortfeasor to partially or fully compensate for the injuries sustained.

FACTS: Helfend (P) sued the RTD (D) for injuries sustained in a bus and automobile accident. RTD (D) appealed the damage award, contending the trial court erred in refusing to admit evidence that Helfend (P) had received health insurance payments from his insurance company which paid 80% of his medical bills. RTD (D) argued the recoverable damages should be reduced by the amount of benefits received.

ISSUE: Does the collateral source rule prohibit the introduction of evidence showing compensation for injuries derived from a completely independent source?

HOLDING AND DECISION: (Tobriner, J.) Yes. The collateral source rule prohibits the introduction of evidence of compensation paid to the plaintiff by a source completely independent from the tortfeasor. The rule does not have a punitive basis and no double recovery is realized as the independent source often has subrogation rights. A defendant should not benefit from the plaintiff's circumspect purchase of insurance coverage, and thus evidence of collateral payment is inadmissible. Affirmed.

EDITOR'S ANALYSIS: The court also stated that if the rule were not applied, individuals would not be induced to spread the risk of injury through insurance. Further, the court rejected the argument that the rule did not apply to public entity defendants. Such defendants are no more entitled to wrongly benefit from the plaintiff's insurance coverage than are private defendants.

PRUITT v. ALLIED CHEMICAL CORP.
523 F. Supp. 975 (E.D. Va. 1981).

NATURE OF CASE: Action for damages for interference with business operations.

FACT SUMMARY: Pruitt (P) and others sued Allied (D) for damage to their business from Allied's (D) pollution of various waterways.

CONCISE RULE OF LAW: Recovery may be obtained for damages proximately caused by the defendant's negligence.

FACTS: Pruitt (P) and others who derive their income from the wildlife who grow in the James River and Chesapeake Bay sued Allied (D), contending that Allied (D) polluted those waterways and materially affected the commercial worth of the wildlife. Allied (D) moved to dismiss the causes of action brought by merchants whose business allegedly suffered from the damage to the sea life in that the demand for such decreased due to the pollution. Allied (D) contended there was no direct injury to any property right held by those plaintiffs.

ISSUE: May recovery be obtained for damages proximately caused by the defendant's negligence?

HOLDING AND DECISION: (Merhige, J.) Yes. Recovery may be obtained for damages proximately caused by the defendant's negligence. In this case, while the injuries to the merchants may have been caused by and even foreseeable from the pollution, it is necessary to place a reasonable, if somewhat arbitrary limit on the recoverable damages. Granting recovery to the merchants as well as the fishermen would require Allied (D) to pay twice for the same injury. Thus, the more direct injury, that of the fishermen, must be recognized, while the injury to the merchants must be held not legally recognizable as too distant in the causal chain. Motion to dismiss granted.

EDITOR'S ANALYSIS: This decision has been criticized on several grounds. First, the court recognized the direct causation, yet imposed a limit on liability from the water's edge. Second, it fails to meet the remedial goal of compensating for loss. However, many jurisdictions recognize that liability for foreseeable injury must, in some circumstances, be limited.

NOTES:

EVRA CORP. v. SWISS BANK CORP.
673 F.2d 951 (7th Cir. 1982), cert den. 459 U.S. 1017 (1982).

NATURE OF CASE: Appeal from award of consequential damages.

FACT SUMMARY: Evra (P) sued Swiss Bank (D) for consequential damages caused by the Bank's (D) failure to electronically transfer funds upon Evra's (P) request.

CONCISE RULE OF LAW: A party may not recover consequential damages when such were consequences of the defendant's negligence which were avoidable by the plaintiff.

FACTS: Evra (P), formerly known as Hyman-Michaels, contracted to charter a ship to carry scrap steel to Brazil. The agreement provided that the shipowner could cancel the agreement for late payment. Payment was to be made by deposit in the owner's account in a bank in Switzerland. Evra (P) would make such payments by having its Illinois bank electronically transfer funds through the Swiss Bank Corp. (D), and the Swiss Bank Corp. (D) would deposit the money in the owner's bank. The agreement became very advantageous to Evra (P) as charter rates climbed, and the shipowner unsuccessfully attempted to cancel the agreement due to late payment. The cancellation was ruled improper by an arbitrator due to a lack of notice of intent to cancel. Subsequently, Evra (P) waited until the last minute to order the transfer of funds, and the Illinois Bank telexed the order the day it was due, and the message, although received, was not transcribed and the money was not transferred. The shipowner immediately notified Evra (P) that the agreement was canceled. Evra (P) spent six days attempting to locate the telex, and when unsuccessful, finally reordered the transfer which was rejected by the shipowner. Another arbitration was held and the agreement was canceled. Evra (P) then sued Swiss Bank (D) for negligently causing the loss of the valuable agreement, and for the cost of the arbitration. The district court found for Evra (P), and Swiss Bank (D) appealed, contending Evra (P) had failed to avoid the consequences of the nontransfer by not immediately reordering the transfer.

ISSUE: May a party recover consequential damages when such were consequences of the defendant's negligence which were avoidable by the plaintiff?

HOLDING AND DECISION: (Posner, J.) No. A party may not recover consequential damages when such were consequences of the defendant's negligence which were avoidable by the plaintiff. In this case, the arbitrator who ruled the agreement canceled based his decision on a finding that Evra (P) failed to take all steps necessary to protect itself from cancellation. Had it immediately rewired the funds, the contract may have been upheld. Thus, the cancellation was a consequence which was avoidable by Evra (P) and no recovery may be realized therefore. Reversed.

EDITOR'S ANALYSIS: The court in this case also relied upon the famous case and rule of Hadley v. Baxendale, 156 Eng.Rep.R. 145 (1854), which limits damages to those reasonably foreseeable. While Hadley was a breach of contract case, the court indicated that the recovery of consequential damages in a tort case is closely analogous. Because Swiss Bank (D) had no actual or constructive knowledge of the consequences of the failure to transfer funds, it could not be held liable for them.

NOTES:

SOUTHWESTERN BELL TELEPHONE CO. v. NORWOOD
212 Ark. 763, 207 S.W.2d 733 (1948).

NATURE OF CASE: Appeal from award of consequential damages.

FACT SUMMARY: Norwood (P) sued Southwestern (D), contending the failure to timely answer his call resulted in a delay in contracting the fire department which increased the fire damage to his house.

CONCISE RULE OF LAW: A telephone company is not liable for special damages for failure to furnish connection to a person if it had no notice of the circumstances out of which the damages might arise.

FACTS: Norwood's (P) home caught fire and he was delayed in contacting the fire department due to Southwestern's (D) failure to immediately answer his call and connect him through. Norwood (P) sued, contending the fire damage was more extensive due to this delay. The jury found for Norwood (P), and Southwestern (D) appealed.

ISSUE: Is a telephone company liable for special damages for failure to furnish a connection to a person if it had no notice of the circumstances out of which the damages might arise?

HOLDING AND DECISION: (McHaney, J.) No. A telephone company is not liable for special damages for its failure to furnish connection to a person if it had no notice of the circumstances out of which the damages might arise. No evidence was presented to establish that Southwestern (D) had undertaken to indemnify Norwood (P) for any speculative damages arising out of the telephone service. Thus, in the absence of such undertaking and in the absence of any foreseeability, the damages here were not recoverable. Reversed.

DISSENT: (Robins, J.) Telephone service is available only from the defendant, and thus a duty of reasonable care in service is required. That duty was breached here, and damages should have been recoverable.

CONCURRENCE: (McFadden, J.) The damages here were not proximate results of the negligence committed. Thus, no recovery is available.

EDITOR'S ANALYSIS: The court here pointed out that because the telephone service contract called for such a small amount from Norwood (P), it would have been unjust to infer that Southwestern (D) undertook the risk of any damages occasioned by the alleged breach. Thus, on either contract or tort grounds, no recovery was available.

BIGELOW v. RKO RADIO PICTURES
327 U.S. 251 (1946).

NATURE OF CASE: Appeal from award of damages for violation of Sherman Act.

FACT SUMMARY: RKO (D) contended Bigelow (P) could not show damages with sufficient certainty to recover for violation of the Sherman Act.

CONCISE RULE OF LAW: A jury may make a just and reasonable estimate of damages based on the evidence presented, and its award need not be based on precise mathematical computations.

FACTS: Bigelow (P) sued RKO (D) and others, contending they had engaged in a discriminatory system of film distribution which violated the Sherman Antitrust Act. The jury awarded damages, which were trebled, based upon evidence of the difference in profitability between Bigelow's (P) theater and a theater which was not a victim of the discrimination. RKO (D) appealed, contending the damage award was not sufficiently certain as the basis was not a precise measuring tool. The appellate court reversed, and the Supreme Court granted certiorari.

ISSUE: Must a damage award be based upon precise mathematical calculations?

HOLDING AND DECISION: (Stone, C.J.) No. A jury may make a just and reasonable estimate of damages based upon the evidence presented, and its award need not be based on precise mathematical calculations. In this case, it could not be established precisely what Bigelow's (P) profit would have been in the absence of the discriminatory practices. The comparison used offered a reasonable method of estimating damages and should be upheld. Reversed.

DISSENT: (Frankfurter, J.) In the absence of proof of actual injury, no violation of the Sherman Act can be found.

EDITOR'S ANALYSIS: This case illustrates the requirement that damages be sufficiently certain to be recoverable. The court noted that it has long been recognized that where the reason for the uncertainty is the act of one party, the issue is resolved in the other party's favor. This holds true in this case where the discriminatory enterprise caused the uncertainty.

BRUNSWICK CORP. v. PUEBLO BOWL-O-MAT
429 U.S. 577 (1977).

NATURE OF CASE: Appeal from reversal of award of damages for violations of anti-trust laws.

FACT SUMMARY: Pueblo (P) sued Brunswick (D), contending the latter's acquisition of bowling centers violated the federal antitrust laws, requiring treble damages and an order of divestiture.

CONCISE RULE OF LAW: Antitrust relief is not available in every case in which a large corporation takes over smaller businesses and causes readjustments in the market share of other participants.

FACTS: Pueblo (P), the owner of several bowling centers, sued Brunswick (D), contending that by acquiring and operating bowling centers which otherwise would have gone bankrupt, Brunswick (D) had brought its deep pocket into the industry and decreased Pueblo's (P) profits. Pueblo (P) contended that it was damaged by the amount of profit it would have realized if the centers were allowed to close down. The trial court granted treble damages and enjoined further acquisitions by Brunswick (D). The court of appeals reversed and remanded, and the Supreme Court granted certiorari.

ISSUE: Is antitrust relief available in every case in which a large corporation takes over smaller businesses and causes readjustments in the market share of other participants?

HOLDING AND DECISION: (Marshall, J.) No. Antitrust relief is not available in every case in which a large corporation takes over smaller businesses and causes readjustments in the market share of other participants. An opposite rule would allow the imposition of antitrust relief in situations not within the general policy underlying the statutes. Every merger potentially causes market share readjustments. Because no anticompetitive effect was shown, no relief is available. Vacated and remanded.

EDITOR'S ANALYSIS: In any type of case, remedial goals are intended to further substantive policy. The province of the judiciary is to shape remedies to further such goals. Thus each violation of substantive law should have a remedy shaped to discourage future violations and compensate for the present violation.

NOTES:

BEAGLE v. VASOLD
417 P.2d 673 (Cal. 1966).

NATURE OF CASE: Appeal from an award of damages for personal injury.

FACT SUMMARY: Beagle's (P) attorney was not allowed to argue to the jury regarding the amount of pain and suffering damages that Beagle (P) should receive in a personal injury action.

CONCISE RULE OF LAW: Attorneys may argue that pain and suffering damages should be computed on a per diem basis.

FACTS: Beagle (P) was riding as a passenger in a car driven by Vasold (D) when he was injured in an accident. Beagle (P) brought a suit against Vasold (D) for loss of earnings, medical expenses, and $61,025 in general damages for pain and suffering. The trial court informed Beagle's (P) attorney that he would not be permitted to inform the jury of the amount sought by Beagle (P) for pain and suffering, nor could he argue that damages should be imposed on a per diem basis. The jury awarded Beagle (P) $1,719. Beagle (P) appealed the judgment as inadequate and asserted that it was error to prohibit counsel from arguing before the jury the amount of damages that should be awarded for pain and suffering.

ISSUE: May attorneys argue that pain and suffering damages should be computed on a per diem basis?

HOLDING AND DECISION: (Mosk, J.) Yes. Regarding damages for pain and suffering, attorneys may argue that they should be computed on a per diem basis. One of the most difficult tasks facing a jury in a personal injury case is determining the amount that should be awarded for pain and suffering. No method is available for such a computation, and it cannot be ascertained with any demonstrable accuracy. The states are split as to whether attorneys may argue that the amount may be measured in terms of a stated number of dollars for a specific period of time. This per diem argument is allowed in a majority of jurisdictions and is favored by commentators who have written on the subject. While it is undeniable that the argument of an attorney does not constitute evidence, the suggestion of a sum for damages can have foundation in the evidence. It is necessarily inferred from observation of the plaintiff and expert testimony regarding the extent and nature of the injuries. If the jury must make such an inference, there is no justification for prohibiting attorneys from making an argument on this issue. Although there may be some slight danger of excessive awards, the verdict must still meet the test of reasonableness. Of course, defense counsel may make any counterarguments on the issue. The per diem argument is a double-edged sword with equal availability and utility to the defendant. Since it is reasonably probable that the award to Beagle (P) would have been more favorable if his attorney had been allowed to argue regarding the amount of pain and suffering damages, the judgment is reversed and remanded for a new trial.

CONCURRENCE: (Traynor, J.) Counsel should be permitted to make any reasonable argument regarding the amount of pain and suffering damages, but the use of any mathematical formula is so misleading because there is no basis in human experience for testing its reasonableness.

EDITOR'S ANALYSIS: Currently, approximately fifteen states permit per diem arguments by counsel, and seven states permit them with a cautionary instruction. Fourteen states forbid the practice altogether. For a discussion of the argument against allowing per diem arguments, see Botta v. Brunner, 138 A.2d 713 (N.J. 1958).

NOTES:

ETHERIDGE v. MEDICAL CENTER HOSPITALS
376 S.E.2d 525 (Va. 1989).

NATURE OF CASE: Appeal of a judgment for damages in a negligence action for personal injury.

FACT SUMMARY: Wilson (P) was severely injured due to the negligence of Medical Center Hospitals (D), but the jury's award of damages was reduced pursuant to a statutory limitation on the amount recoverable for medical malpractice.

CONCISE RULE OF LAW: Statutory limitations on the amount of recovery for medical malpractice are constitutional.

FACTS: In 1980, Wilson (P) underwent surgery at Medical Centers Hospital (D) to restore a deteriorating jawbone. Due to Medical Center's (D) negligence, Wilson (P) suffered severe injuries. She was brain damaged with limited memory and confined to a wheelchair. Etheridge (P), a representative for Wilson (P), brought suit against Medical Centers (D) and proved economic losses in excess of $1.9 million, including lost earnings and medical expenses. The jury awarded a verdict for $2.75 million against Medical Centers (D) and the doctor (D). The trial court applied the recovery limit set for medical malpractice in Code § 8.01-581.15 and reduced the award to $750,000. Wilson (P) appealed, contending that § 8.01-581.15 violated due process and the right to trial by jury.

ISSUE: Are statutory limitations on the amount of recovery for medical malpractice constitutional?

HOLDING AND DECISION: (Stephenson, J.) Yes. Statutory limitations on the amount of recovery for medical malpractice are constitutional. The Virginia Constitution provides for a right to trial by jury. Although a jury's province includes the right to ascertain facts and assess damages, it is the duty of the court to apply the law to the facts. The limitation on medical malpractice recoveries contained in Code § 8.01-581.15 does nothing more than establish the outer limits of a remedy, which is a matter of law. Thus, the application of the limit does not restrict the right to a trial by jury. Substantive due process tests the reasonableness of a statute against the legislature's power to enact the law under the Constitution. Unless a statute restricts a fundamental right, the rational basis test is appropriate. A person has no fundamental right to a particular remedy or to a full recovery in tort actions. A statutory limitation on malpractice remedies is simply an economic regulation which is entitled to judicial deference. The purpose of Code § 8.01-581.15 is to maintain adequate health care services by ensuring that health care providers can obtain affordable malpractice insurance. Thus, the statute has a reasonable relation to a legitimate public purpose and must be upheld. Therefore, the award to Wilson (P) is affirmed.

DISSENT: (Russell, J.) The medical malpractice recovery cap violates the prohibition against special laws contained in the Virginia Constitution. Health care providers should not be singled out as a special class entitled to privileges in tort actions.

EDITOR'S ANALYSIS: The majority contended that the statute's classification was not arbitrary and bore a reasonable and substantial relation to the purpose of the law and, therefore, was not special in effect. Other courts have ruled that similar statutory limitations on remedies were unconstitutional. See Smith v. Department of Insurance, 507 So. 2d 1080 (Fla. 1987).

NOTES:

SMITH v. DEPARTMENT OF INSURANCE

507 So. 2d 1080 (Fla. 1987).

NATURE OF CASE: Appeal from denial of declaratory judgment action.

FACT SUMMARY: Smith (P) sought a ruling that § 59 of the Florida Tort Reform and Insurance Act of 1986 that limited damages for noneconomic losses was unconstitutional.

CONCISE RULE OF LAW: A statutory limitation on damages for noneconomic losses violates the Florida Constitution.

FACTS: Florida enacted the Tort Reform and Insurance Act of 1986, which included a limitation on damages for noneconomic losses. Section 59 of the Act placed a $450,000 limitation on damages to compensate for pain and suffering, physical impairment, mental anguish, and loss of capacity for enjoyment of life. Smith (P) sought a judgment declaring § 59 unconstitutional based upon Article I, § 21 of the Florida Constitution. Section 21 provides that "[t]he courts shall be open to every person for redress of any injury, and justice shall be administered without sale, denial or delay." The trial court upheld § 59, and Smith (P) appealed.

ISSUE: Does a statutory limitation on damages for noneconomic losses violate the Florida Constitution?

HOLDING AND DECISION: (Per curiam) Yes. A statutory limitation on damages for noneconomic losses violates the Florida Constitution. When the Florida Constitution was adopted, there existed the right to sue on and recover noneconomic damages of any amount. The right to redress of any injury does not draw any distinction between economic and noneconomic damages. Furthermore, the language of § 21 does not contain any language that suggests the right may be limited to suits below a certain monetary amount. Although § 59 does not totally eliminate access to the courts, the legislature may not limit the redress of injuries by setting arbitrary caps. Since the right to redress is a constitutional right, it may not be abrogated absent a showing of overpowering public necessity and a lack of alternative methods to meet that necessity. The purpose of assuring available and affordable insurance coverage has not been shown to be a public necessity. Therefore, § 59 is unconstitutional because it violates the constitutional right to redress of injuries without legal justification. Reversed.

EDITOR'S ANALYSIS: Nearly all states have passed varying forms of legislation which has attempted to limit recovery in tort actions. Section 59 applied to all personal injury actions and therefore would not be subject to arguments that it discriminates against certain tort victims, such as the one made by the dissent in Etheridge v. Medical Center Hospitals, 376 S.E.2d 525 (Va. 1989). The statute at issue in Etheridge imposed a cap on medical malpractice damages only.

NOTES:

LEVKA v. CITY OF CHICAGO
748 F.2d 424 (7th Cir. 1984).

NATURE OF CASE: Motion for judgment n.o.v., new trial, or remittitur from civil rights verdict.

FACT SUMMARY: The City of Chicago (D) appealed from a decision denying its motion for judgment n.o.v., or alternatively for a new trial or remittitur, from a verdict rendered in Levka's (P) civil rights action, contending the circumstances attendant to the strip search which formed the basis of Levka's (P) suit did not justify the $50,000 verdict.

CONCISE RULE OF LAW: A court may exercise its discretion in reducing a jury verdict when the evidence indicated the verdict is grossly excessive.

FACTS: Levka (P) brought a civil rights action to recover for a violation of her civil rights she claimed occurred when Chicago police (D) subjected her to a strip search. The search was conducted by matrons, and every arrestee was subjected to such a search by policy. There was only a visual inspection, conducted privately. When Levka (P) protested, she was told "just do it." She testified she felt debased and humiliated, and she called several witnesses to support her claims. Chicago (D) called several witnesses to refute Levka's (P) damages allegations. The jury awarded Levka (P) $50,000, solely for mental anguish, humiliation, embarrassment, etc., and nothing on her claims for lost earnings or loss of earning capacity. Chicago (D) challenged the award as excessive, moving for a judgment n.o.v., or in the alternative, for a new trial or a remittitur. From a denial of its motion, Chicago (D) appealed.

ISSUE: Can a court exercise its discretion in reducing a jury verdict when the evidence indicates the verdict is grossly excessive?

HOLDING AND DECISION: (Pell, J.) Yes. The court may exercise its discretion in reducing a jury verdict when the evidence indicates the verdict is grossly excessive. Such indications are present in this case. The verdict is on the high end of verdicts rendered in similar cases. Further, aggravating circumstances in these other cases, such as vaginal or rectal probing, verbal abuse, etc., which justified a higher verdict, are not present here. This was a relatively straightforward visual strip search, done as privately as possible. Further, Chicago (D) was able to submit evidence sufficient to disallow Levka's (P) earnings claims. Deference to the jury is substantial, but, while not intending to minimize Levka's (P) humiliation, a verdict essentially punitive in nature cannot stand. The award is grossly excessive and subject to reduction. Reversed; vacated; and remanded with instructions.

EDITOR'S ANALYSIS: One of the cases referred to in the decision with a verdict higher than the present case was also reduced on appeal. The fact that Levka (P) was asserting constitutional claims was not essential and does not generally enhance one's ability to resist a motion for remittitur.

NOTES:

CAREY v. PIPHUS
435 U.S. 247 (1978).

NATURE OF CASE: Appeal in action for denial of due process.

FACT SUMMARY: Carey (P), whose procedural due process was denied by his suspension from school without a proper hearing, sought damages.

CONCISE RULE OF LAW: Absent proof of actual injury caused by a denial of procedural due process, only nominal damages may be awarded.

FACTS: Carey (P) was suspended from school without the proper procedural safeguards being taken. He sued under 42 U.S.C. § 1983, alleging that his Fourteenth Amendment right had been violated. The district court found that due process had been denied but declined to award damages since Carey (P) had not submitted evidence showing that he was so entitled. On appeal, the seventh circuit held that the lower court should have heard evidence regarding the damages suffered by Carey (P), but that compensatory damages would not be recoverable for missed school time if the school (D) could show that the student would have been suspended even if a proper hearing had been held; i.e. there was just cause for the suspensions. However, even if just cause was found, Carey (P) would be entitled to recover substantial nonpunitive damages merely because of the denial of his due process, even if no proof is submitted as to the injuries thereby incurred. The Supreme Court granted certiorari.

ISSUE: May substantial damages be awarded for a denial of procedural due process, absent proof of actual injury?

HOLDING AND DECISION: (Powell, J.) No. In many ways, a deprivation of a right under § 1983 creates a liability similar to traditional tort liability. As such, the court of appeals was correct in holding that damages for the deprivation of the substantive right, in this case the missed school time, can only be awarded where actual injury is evidenced in the record. Furthermore, the Court correctly asserted that in any case, if the School (D) shows that the suspension was for good cause, no injury can be found to have flowed from the denial of a hearing in this regard and therefore no damages are to be awarded. However, Carey (P) validly maintains that the denial of procedural due process is an injury, in and of itself. But the court of appeals incorrectly held that this deprivation may be compensated, without proof of actual damages suffered, by substantial damages. There is no basis for this holding. Absent proof of actual injury caused by a denial of procedural due process, only nominal damages may be awarded. Affirmed as modified.

EDITOR'S ANALYSIS: The issue of the kind of damages which may be awarded and the levels of proof required in suits for violations of constitutional rights was discussed thoroughly in Basista v. Weir, 340 F.2d 74 (3rd Cir. 1964). In Basista, the plaintiff was suing for injuries allegedly caused by unconstitutional beatings administered by police officers. The court acknowledged that 42 U.S.C. § 1983 was not specific as to the type of damages allowed for violations. However, after examining the section's history and analogizing to similar statutes, it was held that both compensatory and punitive damages could be recovered. Finally, the court stated that nominal damages automatically flow from the deprivation of a § 1983 right and specific injury need not be proven. Once nominal damages are awarded, punitive damages may also be granted. Apparently, the majority of the states are not in accord with the federal rule as enunciated in Basista. See Hilbert v. Roth, 395 Pa. 270 (1959).

NOTES:

NORFOLK AND WESTERN RAILWAY v. LIEPELT
444 U.S. 490 (1980).

NATURE OF CASE: Appeal from exclusion of evidence and refusal to instruct jury.

FACT SUMMARY: Liepelt's (P) decedent was killed by the negligence of Norfolk (D), his employer, and Norfolk (D) challenged the award of $775,000 in damages on the ground that the jury must have believed the award would be subject to federal income taxation, a matter about which the judge refused evidence and to instruct the jury.

CONCISE RULE OF LAW: It Is error for a trial judge to refuse to admit evidence of the nontaxability of jury awards or to instruct the jury thereof.

FACTS: Liepelt (P) represented a fireman killed through the negligence of his employer, Norfolk (D). After trial on the matter, the jury awarded Liepelt (P) $775,000, though calculation by the decedent's life expectancy and expected salary would have placed the actual loss at approximately $302,000. Norfolk (D) appealed, challenging the award on the ground that the jury must have believed that the award would be subject to federal income taxation in order to have rendered so large a verdict, and that the trial judge refused to hear evidence on taxation and to instruct the jury regarding the freedom of jury awards from income taxation under the Internal Revenue Code. The appellate court found no error, and the Illinois Supreme Court denied hearing. The U.S. Supreme Court granted certiorari.

ISSUE: Is it error for a trial judge to refuse to admit evidence of the nontaxability of jury awards or to instruct the jury thereof?

HOLDING AND DECISION: (Stevens, J.) Yes. In the past, the tax liabilities that a person would incur in the future was regarded as too speculative for a jury to consider in calculating future earning power. The practical wisdom of the trial bar and the trial bench has developed effective methods of presenting essential elements of expert calculations in an understandable form. Despite today's increased general awareness of the realities of taxation, many are surely unaware that jury awards are nontaxable. Thus, it is error for a trial judge to refuse to admit evidence of the nontaxability of jury awards or to instruct the jury thereof. Reversed and remanded.

EDITOR'S ANALYSIS: Traditionally, no evidence was permitted as to the tax consequences of receipt of a jury award. The speculation and the complexity of the calculations required are attenuated by increased familiarity with tax law, and the practical effect of taxation is today far greater than in the past.

NOTES:

CAVNAR v. QUALITY CONTROL PARKING
Tx. Sup. Ct. 696 S.W.2d 549 (1985).

NATURE OF CASE: Review of order denying prejudgment interest in an action for wrongful death, loss of affection, and pain and anguish.

FACT SUMMARY: Cavnar (P) contended that prejudgment interest should be awarded in a wrongful death action.

CONCISE RULE OF LAW: Prejudgment interest may be awarded to a prevailing plaintiff in a personal injury action on damages that have accrued by the time of judgment.

FACTS: Kathy Cavnar's (P) mother was killed when a valet employed by Quality Control Parking (D) intentionally struck her with a motor vehicle. Kathy Cavnar (P) and her siblings sued for loss of affection. The decedent's estate filed a survival action. A jury returned a verdict awarding the children damages for past and future loss of affection, the estate survival damages, and punitive damages as well. The trial court declined to award prejudgment interest.

ISSUE: Should prejudgment interest be awarded in a personal injury action on accrued damages?

HOLDING AND DECISION: (Gonzalez, J.) Yes. Prejudgment interest should be awarded in a personal injury action on damages that have accrued by the time of judgment. The usual rationale for not awarding interest in personal injury cases is that damages are not ascertained until the time of judgment. This court rejects this reasoning, as various actions exist in which damages are not ascertained prior to judgment but do provide for prejudgment interest. An example is contract actions without liquidated damages provisions. Consequently, the rule regarding prejudgment interest in personal injury cases should be the same as that in other types of actions, i.e., that it is awardable. However, only monies for past damages may collect interest, not punitive or future damages. Interest is to begin accruing as of six months after the date of injury in injury cases, and as of the time of death in death cases. Reversed and remanded.

EDITOR'S ANALYSIS: Prejudgment interest reflects the rather elementary economic notion that a dollar today is more valuable than a dollar tomorrow. Since compensatory damages cover periods prior to judgment, full compensation must involve interest. Most states have statutory interest schedules to guide courts in fashioning awards.

JONES AND LAUGHLIN STEEL CORP. v. PFEIFER
462 U.S. 523 (1983).

NATURE OF CASE: Appeal from award for future damages.

FACT SUMMARY: The district court held as a matter of law that in calculating an award of future damages that future inflation is presumed to equal future interest rates, and therefore these factors were offsetting.

CONCISE RULE OF LAW: Federal courts may choose the manner in which to discount the present value of future earnings and are not bound by a rule of state law.

FACTS: Pfeifer (P) was injured in the course of his employment with Jones (D). The district court neither increased the award for future lost earnings to reflect inflation, nor discounted it to reflect its present value, holding it was bound by a Pennsylvania state court decision which held that future inflation and future interest rates are presumed to be equal and the factors are offsetting. Pfeifer (P) appealed, contending the federal court was not bound by state law. The court of appeals affirmed, and the Supreme Court granted certiorari.

ISSUE: May federal courts choose the method to discount future earnings without being bound by state law?

HOLDING AND DECISION: (Stevens, J.) Yes. Federal courts may choose the manner in which to discount the value of future earnings. They are not bound by a rule of state law. There are several acceptable methods of calculating the present value of an award of future damages. Among these are to discount the award according to a market or real interest rate or to predict inflation and discount by a market interest rate. No matter which method is used, no exact figure can be arrived at with precision. Therefore, to adopt a single method as a federal rule of decision would be unworkable. Whatever method is used, the federal court is free to choose it and is not bound by a state rule of decision. Reversed and remanded.

EDITOR'S ANALYSIS: This case illustrates the various methods available to courts to determine the present value of a lump sum award for future damages. The Court recognizes that the fluctuating nature of inflation renders any method used inexact. Because of this, some methods are more appropriate in some cases than in others, and it would not be beneficial to adopt a single method as a rule of decision applicable to all cases.

injunction - 4 factors
irreparable harm
- likelihood of success on merits
- ripeness fails on p-equity forms?
- hardship

CHAPTER 3
PREVENTIVE HARM: THE MEASURE OF INJUNCTIVE RELIEF

QUICK REFERENCE RULES OF LAW

irreparable harm

1. **Preventive Injunctions.** A preliminary injunction will not issue absent a substantial likelihood of irreparable harm. (Humble Oil & Refining Co. v. Harang)

scope of injunctive relief

2. **Preventive Injunctions.** The scope of injunctive relief should not be broader than the evidence warranting it. (Marshall v. Goodyear Tire & Rubber Co.)

ability of recurrent violations needed

3. **Preventive Injunctions.** For a permanent injunction to issue, there must be some cognizable danger of recurrent violations. (United States v. W.T. Grant Co.)

Anticipatory claims ≠ injunctive relief

4. **Preventive Injunctions.** Equity will not grant injunctive relief where land use is reasonable and the plaintiff is alleging the fear of future actions as its grounds for injunctive relief. (Nicholson v. Connecticut Half-Way House)

5. **Reparative Injunctions.** A telephone company is not liable for special damages for failure to furnish connection to a person if it had no notice of the circumstances out of which the damages might arise. (Bell v. Southwell)

Unfair Competition

6. **Reparative Injunctions.** Unfair competition should be enjoined for the amount of time it would take to develop a similar product after public disclosure thereof. (Winston Research Corp. v. Minnesota Mining & Manufacturing Co.)

Investment enterprise.

7. **Reparative Injunctions.** A court may order the liquidation of an investment enterprise when necessary to protect investors. (Bailey v. Proctor)

8. **The Reach of the Injunction When Issued.** A court may make such remedial orders as are necessary to eliminate the results of educational segregation. (Swann v. Charlotte-Mecklenburg Board of Education)

9. **The Reach of the Injunction When Issued.** A district court may not fashion a remedy for segregation in one school district which involves other districts. (Milliken v. Bradley)

10. **The Reach of the Injunction When Issued.** A court may place limits on certain types of punishments which are not per se unconstitutional. (Hutto v. Finney)

11. **The Reach of the Injunction When Issued.** A federal court may order government authorities to obtain funds to pay for court-ordered desegregation by raising taxes. (Missouri v. Jenkins)

12. **Modifying Injunctions.** A party seeking a modification of a consent decree must establish that a significant change in facts or law warrants revision of the decree and that the proposed modification is suitably tailored to the changed circumstance. (Rufo v. Inmates of the Suffolk County Jail)

13. **The Rights of Third Parties.** A court may order a housing authority to correct segregation it has facilitated over an area outside the locality in question. (Hills v. Gautreaux)

14. **The Rights of Third Parties.** A party not violating antidiscrimination laws may not be assessed a share of the costs of implementing a decree remedying the discrimination of others. (General Building Contractors Association v. Pennsylvania)

HUMBLE OIL & REFINING CO. v. HARANG
262 F.Supp. 34 (E.D.La. 1966).

NATURE OF CASE: Petition for preliminary injunction preventing the destruction of certain documents.

FACT SUMMARY: Humble Oil (P), having brought suit against Harang (D), sought an injunction preventing Harang (D) from destroying certain documentary evidence.

CONCISE RULE OF LAW: A preliminary injunction will not issue absent a substantial likelihood of irreparable harm.

FACTS: Harang (D) developed a scheme where in an employee of Humble Oil (P) would reveal to him the sites of Humble's (P) planned drillings, whereupon Harang (D) would acquire an interest in the property and profit therefrom. Upon discovering the scheme, Humble Oil (P) brought a lawsuit against Harang (D). Humble Oil (P) sought a preliminary injunction preventing the destruction of relevant evidence. No evidence was introduced to show a likelihood of document destruction.

ISSUE: Will a preliminary injunction issue absent a likelihood of irreparable harm?

HOLDING AND DECISION: (Rubin, J.) No. A preliminary injunction will not issue absent a likelihood of irreparable harm. The possibility of irreparable harm is not enough; a showing that the irreparable actually will occur is needed. Here, all that was shown was an abstract possibility that document destruction could occur. This is a possibility in every case in which documents constitute evidence. No showing that such destruction was likely to occur was made, and an injunction cannot issue without such a showing.

EDITOR'S ANALYSIS: By obtaining an injunction, Humble Oil (P) was attempting to invoke the contempt power of the court. Violating an injunction constitutes contempt, which can be criminally sanctioned. One has to wonder, however, whether a court order against one in the position of Harang (D) would have greatly influenced his decision-making.

NOTES:

MARSHALL v. GOODYEAR TIRE & RUBBER CO.
554 F.2d 730 (5th Cir. 1977).

NATURE OF CASE: Appeal of permanent injunction prohibiting certain employment practices constituting age discrimination.

FACT SUMMARY: Following a successful suit on behalf of an employee illegally dismissed due to age, the U.S. Labor Dept. (P) obtained a nationwide injunction against Goodyear (D).

CONCISE RULE OF LAW: The scope of injunctive relief should not be broader than the evidence warranting it.

FACTS: One Reed was discharged due to his age by his employer, Goodyear (D). The U.S. Dept. of Labor (P) brought suit on his behalf. The district court ordered Reed be given back pay and also issued a nationwide injunction barring such practices. No evidence of a nationwide age discrimination policy existed. Goodyear (D) appealed the injunction.

ISSUE: Should the scope of injunctive relief be broader than the evidence warranting it?

HOLDING AND DECISION: (Gewin, J.) No. The scope of injunctive relief should not be broader than the evidence warranting it. Injunctive relief is a drastic remedy, and should not be applied lightly. It should only be granted as is appropriate to remedy the problem at issue in the suit before the court. Here, the discharge of a single employee was at issue, not a nationwide policy. The issuance of a nationwide injunction was far broader in scope than the situation before the court and was, therefore, not appropriate. Reversed.

EDITOR'S ANALYSIS: Drafting an injunction can be quite difficult. F.R.C.P. 65(d) states that injunctions and the reasons therefore must be clearly spelled out. The purpose of such a rule is to force the issuing court to fully think through an injunction before issuing one. As the present case demonstrates, however, the plan does not always work.

NOTES:

UNITED STATES v. W.T. GRANT CO.
345 U.S. 629 (1953).

NATURE OF CASE: Appeal of dismissal of suit for injunctive relief.

FACT SUMMARY: After Hancock (D) resigned certain interlocking directorates, the Government (P) continued to petition for an injunction barring such activities.

CONCISE RULE OF LAW: For a permanent injunction to issue, there must be some cognizable danger of recurrent violations.

FACTS: Hancock (D) was a director of several competing retail giants. Contending that this was in violation of the Clayton Act, the Government (P) brought an action seeking an injunction barring Hancock (D) and the retailing firms from such interlocking directorates. Hancock (D) resigned, although he refused to admit he had been violating the Act. The Government (P) continued to petition for an injunction, contending the danger of future violations existed. The Government (P) introduced no evidence of a plan by Hancock (D) or the retailers to renew the activity. The trial court rejected the petition, and the appellate court affirmed.

ISSUE: For a permanent injunction to issue, must there be some cognizable danger of recurrent violations?

HOLDING AND DECISION: (Clark, J.) Yes. For a permanent injunction to issue, there must be some cognizable danger of recurrent violations. While the voluntary cessation of an illegal activity does not render an action to enjoin it moot, proof that the relief is needed must be shown. More than a possibility must be shown. Here, no evidence that the conduct in question was apt to recur was shown, and therefore the trial court was well within the bounds of its discretion in denying the injunction. Affirmed.

DISSENT: (Douglas, J.) The proclivity of the defendants to engage in anticompetitive practices is fairly clear, and to enjoin such practices would be proper.

EDITOR'S ANALYSIS: Mootness was not an issue here. Even though Hancock (D) resigned, the possibility that the conduct in question might repeat was sufficient to allow the court to retain jurisdiction. As the above demonstrates, the amount of proof necessary to avoid mootness and the amount necessary to justify relief are not at all coextensive.

NOTES:

NICHOLSON v. CONNECTICUT HALFWAY HOUSE, INC.
153 Conn. 507 (1966).

NATURE OF CASE: Action to enjoin the use of property.

FACT SUMMARY: Halfway House (D) wanted to use its residential property as a rehabilitation center for paroled convicts.

CONCISE RULE OF LAW: Equity will not grant injunctive relief where land use is reasonable and the plaintiff is alleging the fear of future actions as its grounds for injunctive relief.

FACTS: Connecticut Halfway House (D) purchased a large home in a residential area. It (D) planned to use the home to rehabilitate and counsel paroled felons. Adjoining landowners sought injunctive relief. They alleged that the intended use might increase the crime rate in the area and that it would detrimentally affect property values. The court granted the injunction.

ISSUE: Where the intended use is legal and the only injury claimed is the fear of future actions or a decline in property value, can an injunction be issued?

HOLDING AND DECISION: (Thim, J.) No. The test of whether the intended use of private property constitutes a nuisance to other owners is one of reasonableness. A private property owner may not use his property in an unreasonable manner so as to injure his neighbors. Here, Halfway House's (D) intended use is not prohibited by the zoning law. Nicholson (P) and its other neighbors are afraid of the effect it will have on the neighborhood and property values. They (P) feel that crime may increase and their property will decline in value. The fear of future events or actions does not constitute irreparable injury for which equity will grant an injunction. The injury must be real and current. An injunction will not be granted for what may be groundless fears. Nor will it be granted because prospective buyers may have the same fears. Anticipatory claims such as this one are not grounds for injunctive relief. Judgment reversed.

EDITOR'S ANALYSIS: Where the proposed use has known qualities so that a court may conclude that the use is unreasonable, an injunction may be issued. For example, in Brainard v. Town of West Hartford, 140 Conn. 631, the defendant intended to use residential property as a garbage dump. The court held that the action to enjoin this use was not premature. The court felt that the presence of a dump in a residential neighborhood was an unreasonable use since the qualities of a dump were well known to the court and the fears of adjacent owners were not groundless.

SOUTHWESTERN BELL TELEPHONE CO. v. NORWOOD
212 Ark. 763, 207 S.W.2d 733 (1948).

NATURE OF CASE: Appeal from award of consequential damages.

FACT SUMMARY: Norwood (P) sued Southwestern (D), contending the failure to timely answer his call resulted in a delay in contracting the fire department which increased the fire damage to his house.

CONCISE RULE OF LAW: A telephone company is not liable for special damages for failure to furnish connection to a person if it had no notice of the circumstances out of which the damages might arise.

FACTS: Norwood's (P) home caught fire and he was delayed in contacting the fire department due to Southwestern's (D) failure to immediately answer his call and connect him through. Norwood (P) sued, contending the fire damage was more extensive due to this delay. The jury found for Norwood (P), and Southwestern (D) appealed.

ISSUE: Is a telephone company liable for special damages for failure to furnish a connection to a person if it had no notice of the circumstances out of which the damages might arise?

HOLDING AND DECISION: (McHaney, J.) No. A telephone company is not liable for special damages for its failure to furnish connection to a person if it had no notice of the circumstances out of which the damages might arise. No evidence was presented to establish that Southwestern (D) had undertaken to indemnify Norwood (P) for any speculative damages arising out of the telephone service. Thus, in the absence of such undertaking and in the absence of any foreseeability, the damages here were not recoverable. Reversed.

DISSENT: (Robins, J.) Telephone service is available only from the defendant, and thus a duty of reasonable care in service is required. That duty was breached here, and damages should have been recoverable.

CONCURRENCE: (McFadden, J.) The damages here were not proximate results of the negligence committed. Thus, no recovery is available.

EDITOR'S ANALYSIS: The court here pointed out that because the telephone service contract called for such a small amount from Norwood (P), it would have been unjust to infer that Southwestern (D) undertook the risk of any damages occasioned by the alleged breach. Thus, on either contract or tort grounds, no recovery was available.

WINSTON RESEARCH CORP. v. MINNESOTA MINING & MANUFACTURING CO.
350 F.2d 134 (9th Cir. 1965).

NATURE OF CASE: Appeal of injunction in unfair competition action.

FACT SUMMARY: Winston Research (D) developed a tape recorder with characteristics similar to one soon to be produced by Minnesota Mining (P). Winston (D) consisted of Minnesota Mining (P) defectors.

CONCISE RULE OF LAW: Unfair competition should be enjoined for the amount of time it would take to develop a similar product after public disclosure thereof.

FACTS: Minnesota Mining (3M) (P) developed a certain tape recorder. Prior to the recorder's marketing, Winston Research (D) had been formed by several defecting 3M (P) employees. When the intention of Winston Research (D) to market a similar recorder became known, 3M (P) brought an action to enjoin sales of the recorder. The trial court issued an injunction preventing Winston Research (D) from marketing the recorder for two years, which in the court's estimation was the time necessary for a competitor to develop a similar system after public disclosure thereof. Both sides appealed.

ISSUE: Should unfair competition be enjoined for the amount of time it would take to develop a similar product after public disclosure thereof?

HOLDING AND DECISION: (Browning, J.) Yes. Unfair competition should be enjoined for the amount of time it would take to develop a similar product after public disclosure thereof. An injunction of this nature should prevent unjust enrichment and protect trade secrets, but no more. Here, a permanent injunction would go beyond this goal in that Winston Research (D) would be denied the fruits of what normal research and development would produce. An injunction should not serve to chill the creation of new technologies. The approach of the district court was proper. Affirmed.

EDITOR'S ANALYSIS: Permanent injunctions of the nature that 3M (P) wished to obtain in this action are punitive in nature. That is, they do more than compensate the plaintiff. Generally speaking, equity is compensatory, not punitive. Some courts, however, will indulge in punitive injunctions in egregious cases.

NOTES:

BAILEY v. PROCTOR
160 F.2d 78 (1st Cir. 1947).

NATURE OF CASE: Appeal of court-ordered liquidation of investment trust.

FACT SUMMARY: A court ordered the liquidation of a barely-solvent trust organized before the Investment Company Act of 1940.

CONCISE RULE OF LAW: A court may order the liquidation of an investment enterprise when necessary to protect investors.

FACTS: The Aldred Investment Trust had been set up prior to the Investment Company Act of 1940. Its structure was characterized by concentrated decision-making power with the prospect of high profits for the controlling shareholders to the detriment of the other investors. The Trust became insolvent, and a receiver was appointed. The management of the Trust was changed. The Trust became solvent again. Nonetheless, the court issued an injunction liquidating the Trust. Bailey (P) and others in the control group appealed this order.

ISSUE: May a court order the liquidation of an investment enterprise when necessary to protect investors?

HOLDING AND DECISION: (Mahoney, J.) Yes. A court may order the liquidation of an investment enterprise when necessary to protect investors. Insolvency is not a necessary prerequisite to liquidating an investment enterprise. When it appears that the continuation of the enterprise presents a threat to investors, liquidation may be ordered. Here, although new management had been installed, the structural defects in the trust that permitted the problems to arise in the first place still existed, and the court could legitimately conclude that the Trust's termination was necessary to protect noncontrolling investors. Affirmed.

EDITOR'S ANALYSIS: Like injunction, receivership is an equitable remedy. It, like the injunction, finds its origins in the chancery courts of England. Receivership is thus characterized by the flexibility and wide applicability of injunctions and other equitable remedies.

NOTES:

SWANN v. CHARLOTTE-MECKLENBURG BOARD OF EDUCATION
402 U.S. 1 (1971).

NATURE OF CASE: Appeal of court-ordered desegregation plan.

FACT SUMMARY: To remedy a pattern of state-imposed racial segregation, a district court adopted a plan involving altering of attendance zones, racial quotas, and busing.

CONCISE RULE OF LAW: A court may make such remedial orders as are necessary to eliminate the results of educational segregation.

FACTS: A district court found a pattern of deliberate racial segregation in Mecklenburg County, North Carolina. To remedy this, the court adopted a plan submitted by the county school board and a court-appointed expert. The plan included gerrymandered attendance zones, racial quotas in some schools, and busing. This plan was attacked on appeal.

ISSUE: May a court make such remedial orders as are necessary to eliminate the results of educational segregation?

HOLDING AND DECISION: (Burger, C.J.) Yes. A court may make such remedial orders as are necessary to eliminate the results of educational segregation. The essence of equity jurisdiction is the power of the court of equity to mold each decree to the necessities of each case. In the realm of school desegregation, the threshold question is whether or not a pattern of state-imposed segregation has existed. If the answer is yes, then the court has broad powers to adopt such remedial powers as are necessary. Here, the conclusion that segregated educational facilities had existed was not challenged. This being so, the district court was free to fashion remedies as it saw necessary. The remedies adopted, these being gerrymandered districts, limited racial quotas, and busing, were well within the discretion of the court. Affirmed.

EDITOR'S ANALYSIS: As the decision states, once segregation is found, a court is free to adopt remedies as it sees fit. The main question, then, is whether or not segregation in fact exists. For purposes of federal constitutional law, segregation must be the result of state-imposed doctrines, not accidental residential patterns.

NOTES:

MILLIKEN v. BRADLEY
418 U.S. 717 (1974).

NATURE OF CASE: Appeal of district court desegregation plan involving multiple school districts.

FACT SUMMARY: Faced with a practical impossibility of achieving integration within the Detroit school district, a district court ordered a remedy involving adjacent districts.

CONCISE RULE OF LAW: A district court may not fashion a remedy for segregation in one school district which involves other districts.

FACTS: A district court found a deliberate pattern of segregation in the Detroit school district. The court found it impossible to fashion a remedy for this due to housing and attendance patterns. The court therefore fashioned a plan involving school districts from suburban towns. This plan was challenged on appeal.

ISSUE: May a district court fashion a remedy involving multiple school districts for segregation in one district?

HOLDING AND DECISION: (Burger, C.J.) No. A district court may not fashion a remedy involving multiple school districts for segregation in one district. Local control of school systems is a vital tradition in American public education, and any deviation therefrom should not be taken lightly. To fashion a metropolitan school system would remove much local control of public education. To include in such a plan school districts in which no evidence of de jure segregation exists would be an improper usurpation of local authority. A district court's remedial power does not extend so far. Reversed.

DISSENT: (White, J.) The ultimate responsibility for segregation rests with the state, so broad desegregation plans are proper.

DISSENT: (Marshall, J.) Segregation is the result of state action, so any plan within that state is appropriate.

EDITOR'S ANALYSIS: An important element of the decision was a declaration by Chief Justice Burger that "the scope of the violation determines the scope of the remedy." It is unclear exactly what this means. If adjacent school districts are segregated, it is unclear as to whether interdistrict desegregation would be legitimate if the districts were politically independent of each other.

NOTES:

HUTTO v. FINNEY
437 U.S. 678 (1978).

NATURE OF CASE: Appeal of district court order.

FACT SUMMARY: A district court put a 30-day limit on the time a prisoner could be placed in "punitive isolation" in Arkansas prisons.

CONCISE RULE OF LAW: A court may place limits on certain types of punishments which are not per se unconstitutional.

FACTS: Certain elements of the Arkansas penal system were challenged as unconstitutional. One practice was "punitive isolation," a procedure wherein prisoners were crowded into small cells with virtually no amenities and given inadequate food. The district court found that the system, as a whole, constituted an Eighth and Fourteenth Amendment violation. While not finding punitive isolation per se unconstitutional, the court put a 30-day limit on the length of confinement. The State (D) appealed this order. The court of appeals affirmed.

ISSUE: May a court place limits on certain types of punishments which are not per se unconstitutional?

HOLDING AND DECISION: (Stevens, J.) Yes. A court may place limits on certain types of punishments which are not per se unconstitutional. No one aspect of punitive isolation made it unconstitutional. Various factors were involved in the analysis, one of which was length of confinement. It was well within the court's discretion to find confinements of more than 30 days unconstitutional while shorter stays were not. Affirmed.

DISSENT: (Rehnquist, J.) A court should not be allowed to enjoin a prison practice not found to be in violation of the Constitution. It is not remedial in nature.

EDITOR'S ANALYSIS: J. Rehnquist's dissent made the point that this decision was inconsistent with Milliken II. As the dissent pointed out, it seems that the three-step test for an injunction going towards a state institution was not even addressed. It is not clear how much vitality that test still has.

NOTES:

MISSOURI v. JENKINS
U.S. Sup. Ct., 110 S. Ct. 1651

NATURE OF CASE: Review of order mandating state authorities to levy a tax to fund schools subject to discrimination orders.

FACT SUMMARY: A court of appeals ordered the state of Missouri (D) and certain subdivisions thereof to obtain funds to pay for court-ordered desegregation by raising taxes.

CONCISE RULE OF LAW: A federal court may order government authorities to obtain funds to pay for court-ordered desegregation by raising taxes.

FACTS: Public schools in Kansas City, Missouri were found to be segregated, and desegregation was ordered. The school district did not have the funds to comply with the ruling, and voters in Kansas City had rejected every proposal to increase funding since 1969. The district court ordered an income tax increase for those in Kansas City and its suburbs. The court of appeals modified the order, eliminating the income tax hike but removing state restrictions on the district's power to raise funds through taxation. The state (D) petitioned for certiorari.

ISSUE: May a federal court order government authorities to obtain funds to pay for court-ordered desegregation by raising taxes?

HOLDING AND DECISION: (White, J.) Yes. A federal court may order government authorities to obtain funds to pay for court-ordered desegregation by raising taxes. A federal court has broad powers to invalidate state law that interferes with the achievement of constitutionally mandated desegregation. While a federal court may not be able to impose a tax itself, it can invalidate state laws that operate to frustrate compliance with its orders. Here, the court of appeals found state laws respecting tax increases to be frustrating the school district's ability to fund compliance with desegregation orders, so it properly voided those laws. Affirmed.

DISSENT: (Kennedy, J.) State law creates the ability to tax. To strike down state law respecting taxes is to strike down a local entity's power to tax. What the Court has done has been to give district courts the ability to tax, a result at odds with our federal system.

EDITOR'S ANALYSIS: As the opinion states, the district court imposed an income tax to fund its order. The court of appeals found this excessive, and the Supreme Court suggested it would also if confronted by the issue. However, it is questionable if what the Court did approve is any less intrusive on state sovereignty.

NOTES:

33

RUFO v. INMATES OF THE SUFFOLK COUNTY JAIL
112 S.Ct. 748 (1992).

NATURE OF CASE: Appeal of denial of petition to modify a consent decree.

FACT SUMMARY: The sheriff of Suffolk County (P) contended that a consent decree should be modified to allow the double-bunking of inmates in the new facility because of the increase in the population of pretrial detainees.

CONCISE RULE OF LAW: A party seeking a modification of a consent decree must establish that a significant change in facts or law warrants revision of the decree and that the proposed modification is suitably tailored to the changed circumstance.

FACTS: In October 1978, the court of appeals ordered that the Charles Street Jail be closed unless a plan was presented to create a constitutionally adequate facility for pretrial detainees in Suffolk County. A plan was submitted, and seven months later the district court entered a formal consent decree. Delays of the project ensued, and during that time the inmate population outpaced population projections. The district court modified the decree in 1985 to allow for an increase in the number of cells. In 1989, while the new jail was still under construction, the sheriff (P) moved to modify the consent decree to allow the double-bunking of male detainees, thereby raising the capacity of the new jail. The district court refused to grant the requested modification, holding that the sheriff (P) had failed to meet the standard of United States v. Swift, 286 U.S. 106 (1932), which stated that nothing less than a clear showing of grievous wrong evoked by new and unforeseen conditions should lead to a change in a consent decree. The court of appeals affirmed. This appeal followed.

ISSUE: Must a party seeking a modification of a consent decree establish that a significant change in facts or law warrants revision of the decree and that the proposed modification is suitably tailored to the changed circumstance?

HOLDING AND DECISION: (White, J.) Yes. A party seeking a modification of a consent decree must establish that a significant change in facts or law warrants revision of the decree and that the proposed modification is suitably tailored to the changed circumstance. Instead of the Swift standard, Federal Rule of Civil Procedure 60(b)(5) should be applied, which provides that a party may obtain relief from a court order when "it is no longer equitable that the judgment should have prospective application.' The public interest and considerations based on the allocation of powers within the federal system require that the district court defer to local government administrators, who have the primary responsibility for elucidating, assessing, and solving the problems of institutional reform, to resolve the intricacies of implementing a decree modification. Vacated and remanded.

CONCURRENCE: (O'Connor, J.) While the lack of resources can never excuse a failure to obey constitutional requirements, it can provide a basis for concluding that continued compliance with a decree obligation is no longer equitable if, for instance, the obligation turns out to be significantly more expensive than anyone anticipated. The court is free, when fully exercising its discretion, to reach the same result on remand. This is a case with no satisfactory outcome; the new jail is simply too small.

DISSENT: (Stevens, J.) It is particularly important to apply a strict standard when considering modification requests that undermine the central purpose of a consent decree. In this action, the entire history of the litigation demonstrated that the prohibition against double celling was a central purpose of the relief ordered by the district court in 1973, of the bargain negotiated in 1979 and embodied in the original consent decree, and of the order entered in 1985, which the sheriff (P) now seeks to modify.

EDITOR'S ANALYSIS: United States v. Swift & Co., 286 U.S. 106 (1932), had been the leading case on this issue for 60 years. It was often ignored or evaded but never repudiated. The Court's interpretation of Rule 60(b)(5) may have been limited to institutional reform cases as evidenced by their holding in Nebraska v. Wyoming, 113 S.Ct. 1689 (1993). In a motion to modify a decree, the Court required Nebraska to show "substantial injuries as the result of new water development in Wyoming. This holding leads one to believe that the rule in Swift is not yet dead.

NOTES:

HILLS v. GAUTREAUX
425 U.S. 284 (1976).

NATURE OF CASE: Appeal of court order compelling desegregation of public housing.

FACT SUMMARY: Having found the Dept. of Housing and Urban Development (HUD) to be subsidizing segregated housing in Chicago, a district court ordered a remedial plan encompassing the metropolitan area.

CONCISE RULE OF LAW: A court may order a housing authority to correct segregation it has facilitated over an area outside the locality in question.

FACTS: HUD had been subsidizing segregated public housing in the city of Chicago. A district court ordered HUD to remedy this situation by subsidizing desegregated housing. The court of appeals entered an order in this regard encompassing areas outside of Chicago. This was challenged on appeal to the Supreme Court.

ISSUE: May a court order a housing authority to correct segregation it has facilitated over an area outside the locality in question?

HOLDING AND DECISION: (Stewart, J.) Yes. A court may order a housing authority to correct segregation it has facilitated over an area outside the locality in question. It is true that a remedy cannot go beyond the scope of a constitutional violation. For that reason, a court cannot include nonviolating local authorities in a remedial plan, as was the case in Milliken I. However, a violation by HUD was shown here, and the court properly formulated a remedial plan involving HUD. The fact that the violations occurred in Chicago and some of the remedial action will take place in the suburbs does not challenge the authority of local political subdivisions, as it is HUD that is being coerced, not the local authorities. Affirmed.

EDITOR'S ANALYSIS: The Court did not discuss the extent to which coercion of HUD constituted coercion of local housing authorities. It seems that this case says that a wrongdoer can be forced to take remedial action affecting third parties to whom a court cannot dictate. It would appear the court has left open a method for courts to side-step Milliken I.

NOTES:

GENERAL BUILDING CONTRACTORS ASSOCIATION v. PENNSYLVANIA

458 U.S. 375 (1982).

NATURE OF CASE: Appeal of injunction against discriminatory union practices.

FACT SUMMARY: A district court enjoined certain discriminatory union practices, and included several nondiscriminating parties within the scope of the injunction.

CONCISE RULE OF LAW: A party not violating antidiscrimination laws may not be assessed a share of the costs of implementing a decree remedying the discrimination of others.

FACTS: The International Union of Operating Engineers had a contract with local employers wherein all hiring was to be done through the local union hall. Certain minorities and the Commonwealth (P) challenged the practices. The district court held the practices discriminatory. The court issued an injunction requiring changes in the hiring system and assessed the costs of this against the union, which had been found to be discriminating, and also against certain employers, which had not been found to be discriminating. The injunction was affirmed on appeal.

ISSUE: May a party not violating antidiscrimination laws be assessed a share of the costs of implementing a decree remedying the discrimination of others?

HOLDING AND DECISION: (Rehnquist, J.) No. A party not violating antidiscrimination laws may not be assessed a share of the costs of implementing a decree remedying the discrimination of others. An injunctive remedy of this nature can go no further than the scope of the violation. Since the employers were not found to be discriminating, a remedy including them exceeds the scope of the violation. Reversed.

CONCURRENCE: (O'Connor, J.) Minor ancillary remedies may include parties not found to be liable for a violation of antidiscrimination laws.

EDITOR'S ANALYSIS: Despite the holding here, it seems clear that in this area third parties can be affected by injunctions issued to prevent or remedy discrimination. The Court in this case would allow minor "ancillary remedies" against an innocent third party. Exactly how minor is minor is an issue future decisions will have to answer.

NOTES:

CHAPTER 4
CHOOSING REMEDIES

Uniqueness of land
money damages not appropriate

QUICK REFERENCE RULES OF LAW

1. **Irreplaceable Losses.** An injunction against the felling of trees on another's property is appropriate. (Pardee v. Camden Lumber Co.)

   Replevin = recover Property

2. **Irreplaceable Losses.** A successful litigant in a replevin action has a right to the subject property, rather than cash. (Brook v. James A. Cullimore & Co.)

   Specific relief not available to a one-sided (though legal) agreement.

3. **Irreplaceable Losses.** Even though a contract may be perfectly legal, entitling both parties to legal relief, equity will not provide specific relief to any party who has driven too hard a bargain or obtained too one-sided an agreement. (Campbell Soup Co v. Wentz)

   specific performance when damages won't suffice

4. **Irreplaceable Losses.** A court will decree specific performance of a personal property contract if the legal remedy is inadequate. (Thompson v. Commonwealth)

   uncertainty of value in Contract.

5. **Irreplaceable Losses.** The point at which breach of contract will be redressable by specific performance lies not in any inherent physical uniqueness of the property but, instead, in the uncertainty of valuing it (Van Wagner Advertising Corp. v. S&M Enterprises)

   Intentional encroachment on land

6. **Undue Hardship.** Courts will not conduct the traditional balancing of equities in deciding whether an injunction should issue to remove encroachment on land where the encroachment is found to have been intentional. (Ariola v. Nigro)

   specific performance in Construction K

7. **Burden on the Court.** Absent special circumstances or a compelling public interest, a court of equity should not order the specific performance of any construction contract in a situation in which it would be impractical to carry out such an order. (Northern Delaware Industrial Development)

   enjoin Speech   no

8. **Reasons of Substantive or Procedural Policy.** A court may not enjoin defamatory speech. (Willing v. Mazzocone)

   but defamation can be enjoined - not Constitutionally protected

9. **Reasons of Substantive or Procedural Policy.** Defamation may be enjoined. (Mazzocone v. Willing)

   Specific Performance of personal service K

10. **Reasons of Substantive or Procedural Policy.** On a terminated personal service contract, equitable relief is available only when a danger of unfair competition or other tortious conduct exists. (American Broadcasting Companies v. Wolf)

    Injunction only if factis met - only damages = money

11. **Preliminary or Permanent Relief.** An injunction will not issue unless the petitioning party can demonstrate irreparable harm and that the equities favor the injunction. (Los Angeles Memorial Coliseum Commission v. National Football League) *+ likelihood of success on merits*

    Status Quo

12. **Preliminary or Permanent Relief.** A preliminary injunction may be framed so as to change the status quo. (Lakeshore Hills v. Adcox)

    Bonds + Prelim. Injunc.

13. **Preliminary or Permanent Relief.** A prevailing defendant is entitled to damages on an injunction bond unless good reason for not awarding damages exists. (Coyne-Delany Co. v. Capital Development Board)

    T.R.O's Ex parte

14. **Preliminary or Permanent Relief.** In the absence of a showing of impossibility, ex parte abridgements of First Amendment rights without notice are improper. (Carroll v. President of Princess Anne)

Injunction/equitable remedies only if legal remedies (money) inadequate

15. **Preliminary or Permanent Relief.** A preliminary injunction is not proper in a wrongful discharge suit. (Sampson v. Murray)

11th Amendment

16. **Prospective or Retrospective Relief.** A federal court cannot fashion an equitable remedy compelling a state to make payments out of its treasury. (Edelman v. Jordan)

PARDEE v. CAMDEN LUMBER CO.
70 W.Va. 68, 73 S.E. 82 (1911).

NATURE OF CASE: Appeal of denial of injunction preventing cutting of timber.

FACT SUMMARY: Pardee (P) brought an action to enjoin Camden Lumber (D) from felling trees on his land.

CONCISE RULE OF LAW: An injunction against the felling of trees on another's property is appropriate.

FACTS: Camden Lumber Co. (D) began felling trees on Pardee's (P) property, without his consent. Pardee (P) brought an action to enjoin the practice. The court, not believing equitable relief appropriate, denied the injunction. Pardee (P) appealed.

ISSUE: Is an injunction against the felling of trees on another's property appropriate?

HOLDING AND DECISION: (Poffenbarger, J.) Yes. An injunction against the felling of trees on another's property is appropriate. Where the legal remedy is inadequate, equity will intervene. Timber cut is plainly not the same thing as a standing tree. Money damages will not restore the appearance of the land. When the destruction of something not amenable to replacement is threatened, equity will intervene. The legal remedy here will not replace the character of Pardee's (P) land, and an injunction is therefore appropriate. Reversed.

EDITOR'S ANALYSIS: The decision of the court focused on the unique nature of land. As the court stated, where land is involved, equity will usually be appropriate. This certainly was correct in this instance, as denuded land is not the same as forest. The court really did not discuss irreparable injury, another prerequisite of equity, but the irreparable (within a lifetime) character of the wrong was obvious here.

NOTES:

BROOK v. JAMES A. CULLIMORE & CO.
Okla. Sup. Ct., 436 P.2d 32 (1967).

NATURE OF CASE: Appeal of court-ordered delivery of personal property.

FACT SUMMARY: Brook (D), liable to James A. Cullimore & Co. (P) for certain collateral, offered instead to deliver cash of equivalent value.

CONCISE RULE OF LAW: A successful litigant in a replevin action has a right to the subject property, rather than cash.

FACTS: Brook (D) borrowed approximately $8,000 from Cullimore (P). Brook (D) gave Cullimore (P) a security interest in certain property valued at around $25,000. Brook (D) defaulted on the note, and Cullimore (P) brought an action to obtain possession of the property. Brook (D) offered cash equivalent to the value of the property. Cullimore (P) refused, desiring the property. The court ordered Brook (D) to deliver the property, and Brook (D) appealed.

ISSUE: Does a successful litigant in a replevin action have a right to the subject property, rather than cash?

HOLDING AND DECISION: (McInerney, J.) Yes. A successful litigant in a replevin action has a right to the subject property, rather than cash. A replevin action is at common law an action to recover property, not money. Statutes have modified replevin to allow for damages if the property is unavailable, but this is at the option of the plaintiff, not the defendant. Here, since Cullimore (P) was successful, it had a right to demand the property itself, not a cash equivalent. Affirmed.

EDITOR'S ANALYSIS: Replevin is a very old remedy, predating equity. As the case indicates, it is employed in cases where delivery of personal property is required. The remedy has some flaws; for instance, hearings are often delayed, and the property can be secreted. Some equitable remedies, such as T.R.O.s, can ameliorate this

NOTES:

CAMPBELL SOUP CO. v. WENTZ
172 F.2d 80 (3d Cir. 1948).

NATURE OF CASE: Appeal from dismissal of breach of contract action for specific relief.

FACT SUMMARY: Wentz (D) contracted to sell carrots to Campbell (P) but instead sold them to Lojeski (D).

CONCISE RULE OF LAW: Even though a contract may be perfectly legal, entitling both parties to legal relief, equity will not provide specific relief to any party who has driven too hard a bargain or obtained too one-sided an agreement.

FACTS: On June 21, 1947, Wentz (D) contracted to sell all the Chantenay red cored carrots to be grown on a certain fifteen-acre parcel of his farm to Campbell (P) for a price between $23 and $30 per ton. The contract, drawn up by and in the primary interest of Campbell (P), provided several conditions. Paragraph 2 set out a very particular manner of delivery and further stated that Campbell (P) was to be judge of conformance with all specifications. Paragraphs 3 and 4 provided that Campbell (P) could refuse all carrots in excess of twelve tons per acre but that Wentz (D) could only sell such excess carrots after Campbell (P) rejected them. Paragraph 9 provided certain circumstances under which Campbell (P) would be excused from accepting delivery of any carrots but provided that, even if it was, Wentz (D) could not sell the carrots elsewhere without Campbell's (P) approval. By January 1948, the price of Chantenay carrots had risen to $90 per ton. Wentz (D) thereupon notified Campbell (P) that it would no longer deliver carrots to them, selling instead to Lojeski (D), a neighbor, who in turn sold to Campbell (P). Campbell instituted this action, as a result, for specific performance of its contract with Wentz (D). The trial court dismissed, and this appea followed.

ISSUE: May a court of equity deny specific relief to a party to a wholly legal contract merely because he has obtained a markedly one-sided agreement?

HOLDING AND DECISION: (Goodrich, J.) Yes. Even though a contract may be perfectly legal, entitling both parties to legal relief, equity will not provide specific relief to any party who has driven too hard a bargain or obtained too one-sided an agreement. The general policy of liberality in the granting of specific relief favors the granting of it as long as the court is not forced to undertake too burdensome or time-consuming a supervisory role in the process. As such, the trial court below erred in dismissing the suit because of the purported adequacy of the legal remedy here. (The relative "uniqueness" of these carrots is really immaterial.) But the dismissal was nevertheless proper considering the excessively burdensome provisional that Campbell (P) obtained in its contract with Wentz (D). Affirmed.

EDITOR'S ANALYSIS: This case points up what has been termed "equity's middle course" in the question of whether courts should enforce contracts which, though unfair, fall short of being unconscionable. Essentially equitable (though not legal) relief will be denied wherever the evidence supports a finding of misrepresentation, unclean hands (from overreaching), inadequate consideration, equitable estoppel, etc. Note also, here, the fact that the court skirts the question of adequacy of the legal remedy which the trial court had held dispositive below. As a general rule, inadequacy of the legal remedy (i.e., damages) must be established before a party may obtain equitable relief. "Uniqueness" of the subject matter of a contract (carrots, above) will often make damages inadequate. In Campbell, the court in essence said that the mere need for product uniformity by Campbell (P) in its soups made Wentz's (D) Chantenay red carrots unique.

NOTES:

THOMPSON v. COMMONWEALTH

197 Va. 208, 89 S.E.2d 64 (1955).

NATURE OF CASE: Appeal from decree of specific performance in action to enforce a contract.

FACT SUMMARY: Virginia (P) brought an action against Thompson (D) and his company to compel compliance with a contract to deliver spare parts for a vote counting system installed by Thompson (D).

CONCISE RULE OF LAW: A court will decree specific performance of a personal property contract if the legal remedy is inadequate.

FACTS: In 1945, Thompson (D) contracted with Virginia (P) to install certain vote counting apparatus in the state legislature and to furnish spare parts. Thompson (D) later reneged on supplying the spare parts, and Virginia (P) brought an action to compel compliance. Evidence showed the parts were not made by any other entity. The trial court decreed specific performance, and Thompson (D) appealed.

ISSUE: Will a court decree specific performance in a personal property contract if the legal remedy is inadequate?

HOLDING AND DECISION: (Smith, J.) Yes. A court will decree specific performance of a personal property contract if the legal remedy is inadequate. Generally contracts involving personal property are not subject to specific performance. This is merely because damages are usually adequate. Where damages are not adequate, specific performance will lie. Here, no other source of the needed spare parts appears to exist, so no alternate way of obtaining them can be found. This being the case, damages will not suffice. Affirmed.

EDITOR'S ANALYSIS: The defendants argued that to compel them to work on the contract was tantamount to involuntary servitude. The court did not buy that argument. As the court pointed out, the defendants had the option of subcontracting the necessary work.

NOTES:

VAN WAGNER ADVERTISING CORP. v. S & M ENTERPRISES

N.Y. Ct. of App., 67 N.Y.2d 186 (1986).

NATURE OF CASE: Appeal from denial of specific performance in breach of contract action.

FACT SUMMARY: Van Wagner (P) contended that S & M's (D) cancellation of a lease of billboard space on the side of a building was ineffective because only an owner making a bona fide sale could terminate the lease, and Van Wagner's (P) lease had not been terminated by the former owner of the building, Michaels, before she sold it to S & M (D).

CONCISE RULE OF LAW: The point at which breach of contract will be redressable by specific performance lies not in any inherent physical uniqueness of the property but, instead, in the uncertainty of valuing it.

FACTS: Michaels leased billboard space on the side of a building she owned to Van Wagner Advertising Corp. (P). Van Wagner (P) erected a sign on the building and leased it to Asch Advertising, Inc. for three years. Michaels sold the building to S & M Enterprises (D), and S & M (D) canceled the lease with Van Wagner (P). Van Wagner (P) sued for specific performance and damages for breach of contract, contending that only an owner making a bona fide sale could terminate the lease, and that Michaels had not terminated the lease before she sold the building to S & M (D). The trial court ruled for Van Wagner (P), stating that the parties did not intend that once a sale had been made that any future purchaser could terminate the lease at will. The court would not, however, order specific performance, and Van Wagner (P) appealed.

ISSUE: Does the point at which breach of a contract will be redressable by specific performance lie not in any inherent physical uniqueness of the property but, instead, in the uncertainty of aluing it?

HOLDING AND DECISION: (Kaye, J.) Yes. The point at which breach of a contract will be redressable by specific performance lies not in any inherent physical uniqueness of the property but, instead, in the uncertainty of valuing it. In stating that the subject matter of a contract is unique and has not established market value, a court is really saying that it cannot obtain, at reasonable cost, enough information about substitutes to permit it to calculate an award of money damages without imposing an unacceptably high risk of undercompensation on the injured promisee. Here, the trial court correctly concluded that the value of the "unique qualities" of the demised space could be fixed with reasonable certainty and without imposing an unacceptably high risk of undercompensating the injured tenant. Thus, the court correctly concluded that specific performance should be denied Van Wagner (P) because such relief would be inequitable in that its effect would be disproportionate in its harm to S & M (D) and in its assistance to Van Wagner (P). Affirmed.

EDITOR'S ANALYSIS: Specific performance is an equitable remedy. Its availability is severely restricted by the necessity of meeting the traditional prerequisite of equitable relief — a showing that the available legal remedies would be inadequate. This most often means that if the contracted-for performance is available from any other source, specific performance will be denied, and plaintiff will have to settle for money damages.

NOTES:

ARIOLA v. NIGRO
16 Ill.2d 46, 156 N.E.2d 536 (1959).

NATURE OF CASE: Appeal from award of damages for injury to property rights.

FACT SUMMARY: The trial court refused to issue an injunction requiring Nigro (D) to remove an encroachment on Ariola's (P) land due to the undue hardship such would cause.

CONCISE RULE OF LAW: Courts will not conduct the traditional balancing of equities in deciding whether an injunction should issue to remove encroachment on land where the encroachment is found to have been intentional.

FACTS: Nigro (D) began construction on his land and laid concrete flush against Ariola's (P) building. Ariola (P) notified him that such was an encroachment on his property and supported such with professional surveys. Nigro (D) continued to build and after construction, Ariola (P) sued for damages and an injunction to force removal of the encroaching structure. The trial court found the encroachment consisted of a matter of inches and upon weighing the equities involved denied the injunction. Ariola (P) was awarded damages for the removal of a rain gutter by Nigro (D), yet the injunction was denied. Both parties appealed.

ISSUE: Will courts weigh equities in determining whether to enjoin an intentional encroachment on land?

HOLDING AND DECISION: (Bristow, J.) No. Courts will not conduct the traditional balancing of equities in deciding whether an injunction should issue to remove encroachments on land where the encroachment is found to have been intentional. In this case Nigro (D) intentionally proceeded in the face of substantial evidence he was encroaching on Ariola's (P) land. Even though he held a good faith belief he was not encroaching he proceeded at his own risk in constructing on the land. Thus, the injunction should have issued. Reversed and remanded.

EDITOR'S ANALYSIS: In the usual case, a balancing of the equities requires the court to evaluate the benefit that the plaintiff will derive from the equitable relief with the detriment such relief will cause the defendant. Often requiring the destruction of an edifice which only slightly encroaches on another's land does not adequately balance the competing interests. Courts of equity seek to do what is most fair to both sides, if possible.

NOTES:

NORTHERN DELAWARE INDUSTRIAL DEVELOPMENT CORP. v. E.W. BLISS CO.
245 A.2d 432 (Del. Ch. 1968).

NATURE OF CASE: Motion for order to compel requisitioning of laborers.

FACT SUMMARY: Northern Delaware (NDIDC) (P) sought an order for equitable relief requesting that E.W. Bliss (D), the firm that contracted to remodernize a steel fabricating plant, hire a second shift of workers so the remodernization would be speeded up.

CONCISE RULE OF LAW: Absent special circumstances or a compelling public interest, a court of equity should not order the specific performance of any construction contract in a situation in which it would be impractical to carry out such an order.

FACTS: NDIDC (P) and E.W. Bliss (D) contracted for the remodernization of a steel fabricating plant owned by Phoenix Steel Corp. (P). A proposal made by E.W. Bliss' (D) prime subcontractor contained a "Working Schedule" provision that contemplated a double shift work schedule when one of the steel mills had to be shut down to carry out the remodernization. Work on the massive project did not proceed as rapidly as originally contemplated, and E.W. Bliss (D) was clearly behind schedule. NDIDC (P) and Phoenix Steel (P) made a motion for equitable relief requesting in essence that, as contemplated in the "Working Schedule," E. W. Bliss (D) be required to hire sufficient laborers to form a night shift during the period that one of the steel mills was shut down in an effort to speed up work on the project. The court noted that there was some question as to the availability of laborers to grant the relief sought.

ISSUE: Absent special circumstances or a compelling public interest, should a court of equity order specific performance of any construction contract in a situation in which it would be impractical to carry out such an order?

HOLDING AND DECISION: (Marvel, V.C.) No. Absent special circumstances or a compelling public interest, a court of equity should not order the specific performance of any construction contract in a situation in which it would be impractical to carry out such an order. In the present situation, the parties have contracted for a massive, complex remodernization, and the contract is nowhere near finished. There is some question as to the availability of laborers to grant the relief requested. There is no question that a court of equity has jurisdiction to grant the relief sought, but in light of the imprecision of the contractual provision being relied on, and the impracticability, if not impossibility, of enforcing the order, specific performance of the provision contemplating the second shift would be inappropriate. NDIDC (P) and Phoenix Steel (P) will be able to sue later for damages resulting from actionable building delays.

EDITOR'S ANALYSIS: While the court's fears in ending up supervising the enforcement of the order may have been premature, they certainly were not groundless. In a situation where the parties are cooperative, supervision might be practically nonexistent. If, however, the parties are noncooperative, the court would, in a situation like the present case, be forced to become involved in every minute detail of the remodernization.

NOTES:

WILLING v. MAZZOCONE

Pa. Sup. Ct., 482 Pa. 377, 393 A.2d 1155 (1978).

NATURE OF CASE: Appeal of injunction prohibiting exhibiting of defamatory sign.

FACT SUMMARY: Willing (D), believing herself to have been defrauded by Mazzocone (D) and his law firm, walked around city hall with a defamatory sign.

CONCISE RULE OF LAW: A court may not enjoin defamatory speech.

FACTS: Willing (D) had been represented by the law firm of Quinn & Mazzocone in a worker's compensation action. Willing (D) formed the belief that Quinn & Mazzocone (P) cheated her. She began walking around the outside of city hall with a placard saying that the firm stole money from her and "sold me out to the insurance company." Quinn & Mazzocone (P) brought an action to enjoin this behavior. The evidence at the hearing indicated that Quinn & Mazzocone (P) had done nothing unethical, and that Willing (D) was either eccentric or mentally ill. The court issued an injunction, and Willing (D) appealed. Willing (D) was indigent.

ISSUE: May a court enjoin defamatory speech?

HOLDING AND DECISION: (Manderino, J.) No. A court may not enjoin defamatory speech. Prior restraints of free speech are repugnant to the American political heritage, and an injunction such as that which issued would undoubtedly be highly suspect from a constitutional standpoint. However, the constitutional issue need not be addressed, because the legal remedy in a defamation is adequate. A suit for libel or slander, if successful, serves to exonerate a party and compensates for actual damages, if any exist. The fact that Willing (D) is indigent is irrelevant. A legal remedy does not become inadequate because it appears uncollectible. Reversed.

CONCURRENCE: (Roberts, J.) Conditioning the propriety of equitable relief on a party's indigence is clearly wrong.

EDITOR'S ANALYSIS: One has to question some aspects of the court's opinion. It would seem that a successful verdict in a libel suit would not, absent some unusual publicity, restore a reputation. Also, to say that an uncollectible legal remedy is adequate is a suspect conclusion. It may be that the court was stretching to avoid discussing the constitutional issues.

NOTES:

MAZZOCONE v. WILLING
Pa. Super. Ct. 369 A.2d 829 (1976)

NATURE OF CASE: Appeal from order enjoining publication of allegedly defamatory material.

FACT SUMMARY: Mazzocone (P) sought an injunction to prevent Willing (D) from demonstrating in front of the courthouse with a sign that read "Law firm of Quinn-Mazzocone stole money from me..."

CONCISE RULE OF LAW: Defamation may be enjoined.

FACTS: Willing (D), a former client of attorney Mazzocone (P), became obsessed with the notion that she had been "sold out" by Mazzocone (P), despite a lack of a reasonable basis for so believing. She began daily demonstrations on the sidewalk outside of the courthouse in which Mazzocone (P) practiced, wearing a "sandwich" sign to the effect that Mazzocone had stolen money from her, all the while pushing a shopping cart and ringing a cowbell. Mazzocone (P) filed an action to enjoin her from displaying the sign. The trial court enjoined her from going near the property and from displaying the sign. Willing (P) appealed.

ISSUE: May defamation be enjoined?

HOLDING AND DECISION: (Cercone, J.) Yes. Defamation may be enjoined. The reasons for holding otherwise do not pass muster. It has been argued that the equitable remedy of an injunction deprives the defendant of having the jury pass on the truth or falsity of the alleged defamation. In borderline cases this may be so, but not here, where the defamation is clear. Another rationale offered against such relief is that damages are an adequate remedy, so equity is unavailable. However, when, as here, reputation is on the line, damages may not make a plaintiff whole. The final and most persuasive argument against enjoining defamation is that it constitutes an abridgement of free speech in violation of the First Amendment. The short answer to this, however, is that the Supreme Court has held that defamation is not constitutionally protected. Consequently, as Mazzocone (P) has no other viable remedy, the injunction was proper. [The court modified the injunction to make it somewhat narrower and then affirmed as modified].

DISSENT: (Jacobs, J.) Without proof of damages, it cannot be said that damages are an inadequate remedy.

EDITOR'S ANALYSIS: The extent to which the Constitution would allow an injunction of this nature depends upon the reach of the First Amendment. In this instance Mazzocone (P) was not a public figure, so the First Amendment would not greatly impact on his right to an injunction. A public figure would have a much tougher time overcoming the First Amendment objection to an injunction, as the Amendment has been interpreted to provide more protection for speech involving public officials.

NOTES:

AMERICAN BROADCASTING COMPANIES v. WOLF
52 N.Y.2d 394, 420 N.E.2d 363 (1981).

NATURE OF CASE: Appeal from denial of restraining order.

FACT SUMMARY: Wolf (D) reneged on a term in his contract with ABC (P) giving ABC (P) a right of first refusal on Wolf's (D) new contract.

CONCISE RULE OF LAW: On a terminated personal service contract, equitable relief is available only when a danger of unfair competition or other tortious conduct exists.

FACTS: Wolf (D) contracted with ABC (P) to provide broadcasting services. A clause in his contract called for ABC (P) to have certain rights of first refusal in negotiations for the next contract. Before the contract expired, Wolf (D) signed a new agreement to work for CBS upon expiration of the ABC (P) contract. ABC (P) brought an action for specific performance of the right of first refusal clause and to enjoin Wolf (D) from working for CBS. The trial court denied this relief, and ABC (P) appealed.

ISSUE: On a terminated personal service contract is equitable relief available only when a danger of unfair competition or other tortious conduct exists?

HOLDING AND DECISION: (Cooke, C.J.) Yes. On a terminated personal service contract equitable relief is available only when a danger of unfair competition or other tortious conduct exists. Public policy in this area favors free competition, so restrictive covenants with respect to personal services will be upheld only when a failure to uphold them presents some sort of threat to the employer. This might occur in the instance of the employee giving away trade secrets. No evidence of any such danger exists here. For this reason, the requested relief was properly denied. Affirmed.

EDITOR'S ANALYSIS: Courts rarely will compel specific performance of a personal service contract. This is due to both administrative and Thirteenth Amendment concerns. If a court wishes to compel a party to perform an employment contract, it will generally enjoin the employee from alternate employment.

NOTES:

LOS ANGELES MEMORIAL COLISEUM COMMISSION v. NATIONAL FOOTBALL LEAGUE
634 F.2d 397 (9th Cir. 1980).

NATURE OF CASE: Appeal of preliminary injunction in antitrust action.

FACT SUMMARY: The Commission (P) sought preliminary injunction barring the NFL (D) from enforcing its rules regarding franchise relocation.

CONCISE RULE OF LAW: An injunction will not issue unless the petitioning party can demonstrate irreparable harm and that the equities favor the injunction.

FACTS: The Oakland Raiders wished to move into the Los Angeles Memorial Coliseum. A potential impediment to this was NFL rule 4.3, which required approval of 75% of the NFL (D) owners. Faced with the prospect of failure to gain approval, the Commission (P) sought an injunction preventing the NFL (D) from enforcing rule 4.3. The Commission (P) was unable to show any potential loss other than pecuniary. Nor did the district court make findings of fact with respect to potential harm to the NFL (D). Nonetheless, the district court issued a preliminary injunction barring the enforcement of rule 4.3. The NFL (D) appealed.

ISSUE: Will an injunction issue if the petitioning party cannot demonstrate irreparable harm and the equities favor the injunction?

HOLDING AND DECISION: (Poole, J.) No. An injunction will not issue unless the petitioning party can demonstrate irreparable harm and that the equities favor the injunction. The basic criteria for a preliminary injunction are a likelihood of success on the merits, irreparable harm, and favorable equities. Here, the Commission (P) could only show possible pecuniary loss; damages can satisfactorily remedy this. Also, no findings regarding possible harm to the NFL (D) were made, so whether the equities favor the injunction is unclear. Reversed.

CONCURRENCE: (Wallace, J.) As irreparable harm is not shown, no more analysis is necessary for reversal.

EDITOR'S ANALYSIS: The criteria for a preliminary injunction vary from state to state. Some courts factor in public policy, others do not. However, most, if not all, require a showing of irreparable harm and a favorable equitable balance.

LAKESHORE HILLS v. ADCOX
Ill. Ct. of App., 90 Ill.App.3d 609, 413 N.E.2d 548 (1980).

NATURE OF CASE: Appeal of preliminary injunction in action to enforce residential deed covenant.

FACT SUMMARY: Lakeshore Hills (P) brought an action to compel Adcox (D) to observe a covenant in a deed prohibiting the keeping of wild animals.

CONCISE RULE OF LAW: A preliminary injunction may be framed so as to change the status quo.

FACTS: Lakeshore Hills (P) was a corporation overseeing the operation of a housing development. When Adcox (D) purchased a lot, a covenant excluded the keeping of animals other than "household pets." Adcox (D) began keeping an adult bear on his property. Although Adcox (D) claimed the bear was harmless, Lakeshore Hills (P) brought an action to compel removal of the bear. The trial court issued a preliminary injunction, and Adcox (D) appealed.

ISSUE: May a preliminary injunction be framed so as to change the status quo?

HOLDING AND DECISION: (Craven, J.) Yes. A preliminary injunction may be framed so as to change the status quo. Preliminary injunctions usually preserve the status quo, but this is not a rule. As long as the criteria of probable success on the merits, no adequate legal remedy, balancing of the equities, and no harm to the public are met, a preliminary injunction changing the status quo is permissible. Here, damages could not suffice to allay fears about the bear, so legal remedies are inadequate. Success on the merits appears likely, and the equities and public interest would seem on the side of Lakeshore (P). Affirmed.

EDITOR'S ANALYSIS: Generally speaking, preliminary injunctions do preserve the status quo. In fact, many jurisdictions do not allow preliminary injunctions changing the status quo. The rule here would appear to be in the minority, although it is perhaps merging.

NOTES:

COYNE-DELANY CO. v. CAPITAL DEVELOPMENT BOARD
717 F.2d 385 (7th Cir. 1983).

NATURE OF CASE: Appeal of denial of damages on a bond issued pursuant to a later-reversed preliminary injunction.

FACT SUMMARY: When a preliminary injunction issued in favor of Coyne-Delany Co. (P) was reversed on appeal, the district court refused to award damages on the injunction bond.

CONCISE RULE OF LAW: A prevailing defendant is entitled to damages on an injunction bond unless good reason for not awarding damages exists.

FACTS: Unhappy with certain valves delivered by Coyne-Delany (P) pursuant to a contract, the Capital Development Board (D) solicited bids for another to supply the valves. Coyne-Delany Co. (P) brought an action to enjoin this, claiming it had a property interest in the contract that had been taken without due process. The district court issued an injunction, and Coyne-Delany Co. (P) put up a $5,000 bond. The injunction was later reversed, as a case came down making the claim invalid. The Capital Development Board (D) asked that its damages be paid out of the bond, and the district court refused, holding the lawsuit to have been brought in good faith. Capital (D) appealed.

ISSUE: Is a prevailing defendant entitled to damages on an injunction bond unless good reason for not awarding damages exists?

HOLDING AND DECISION: (Posner, J.) Yes. A prevailing defendant is entitled to damages on an injunction bond unless good reason for not awarding damages exists. F.R.C.P. 65(c) mandates the posting of a bond to cover a defendant's possible expenses if it prevails. F.R.C.P. 54(d) states that a prevailing party is entitled to its costs. These sections, read together, imply that a defendant is entitled to its damages if it prevails. While a district court has some discretion in making such awards, the discretion is not unfettered. Only when a cause exists for not awarding damages, such as a failure to mitigate, should damages be withheld. The court should not fail to award damages merely because the action was filed in good faith, as was the case here. Reversed.

EDITOR'S ANALYSIS: There appears to be a conflict in the circuits with respect to a district court's discretion in awarding damages on preliminary injunction bonds. The 10th Circuit appears to make it mandatory. The 7th Circuit makes it mandatory in the absence of good cause not to. The D.C. Circuit gives more discretion.

CARROLL v. PRESIDENT OF PRINCESS ANNE
393 U.S. 175 (1968).

NATURE OF CASE: Appeal of temporary restraining order.

FACT SUMMARY: Authorities of the town of Princess Anne (P) obtained an ex parte T.R.O. preventing a political rally.

CONCISE RULE OF LAW: In the absence of a showing of impossibility, ex parte abridgements of First Amendment rights without notice are improper.

FACTS: A white supremacist organization held a political rally filled with potentially inflammatory speech. This was in the town of Princess Anne (P). Upon hearing that another rally was planned for the next day, the authorities obtained an ex parte T.R.O. prohibiting the rally. No notice of the application was given or even attempted. The T.R.O. was obtained. The court later issued an injunction prohibiting rallies for 10 months. The state appellate court reversed the injunction, but allowed the T.R.O. to stand. Carroll (D) and other organization members appealed.

ISSUE: In the absence of a showing of impossibility, are ex parte abridgements without notice of First Amendment rights proper?

HOLDING AND DECISION: (Fortas, J.) No. In the absence of a showing of impossibility, ex parte abridgements of First Amendment rights without notice are improper. It is impossible for a court to intelligently weigh the issues in as delicate a situation as is a First Amendment issue without an adversary hearing. An order must be framed in the narrowest terms possible, and such precise tailoring is impossible without a full hearing. Reversed.

CONCURRENCE: (Douglas, J.) A T.R.O. can never constitutionally restrain speech.

EDITOR'S ANALYSIS: F.R.C.P. 65 provides the parameters of T.R.O.s. The Rule provides that notice must be given or an affidavit explaining the reasons for lack of notice must be presented. This is consistent with the rule of the Court given here.

NOTES:

SAMPSON v. MURRAY
415 U.S. 61 (1974).

NATURE OF CASE: Appeal of an issuance of a preliminary injunction barring termination of employment.

FACT SUMMARY: Murray (P), terminated by the Government (D), filed a wrongful discharge claim and obtained a preliminary injunction compelling the Government (D) to rehire her.

CONCISE RULE OF LAW: A preliminary injunction is not proper in a wrongful discharge suit.

FACTS: Murray (P) was employed by the Federal Government (D). The Government (D) terminated her. Murray (P) filed an action with the Civil Service commission claiming wrongful discharge and also sought an injunction forcing the Government (D) to rehire her. The injunction was issued. The court of appeals affirmed, and the Government (D) appealed.

ISSUE: Is a preliminary injunction proper in a wrongful discharge suit?

HOLDING AND DECISION: (Rehnquist, J.) No. A preliminary injunction is improper in a wrongful discharge suit. It is basic in equitable relief that legal remedies must be inadequate. Wrongful termination can lead to lost income, which is compensable at law. While the argument can be made that a loss of reputation may result from a wrongful discharge, if the claimant prevails, the claimant will be vindicated. The damage therefore will not be irreparable. For this reason, the injunction was improper. Reversed.

DISSENT: (Douglas, J.) Reinstatement may not vindicate the employee's reputation entirely.

DISSENT: (Marshall, J.) No appealable order has been entered, and this court lacks jurisdiction. Turning to the merits, the indignities of wrongful discharge constitute irreparable injury.

EDITOR'S ANALYSIS: The district court called its order a T.R.O., but extended it beyond the 10-day limit of F.R.C.P. 65. For this reason, the Court considered it a preliminary injunction. Justice Marshall did not agree with this, and for that reason argued that no jurisdiction existed.

NOTES:

EDELMAN v. JORDAN
415 U.S. 651 (1974).

NATURE OF CASE: Appeal of injunction ordering welfare payments.

FACT SUMMARY: A district court issued an injunction compelling Illinois to make certain welfare payments to Jordan (P).

CONCISE RULE OF LAW: A federal court cannot fashion an equitable remedy compelling a state to make payments out of its treasury.

FACTS: Illinois participated in a federal program wherein the United States matched certain welfare payments if the participating state agreed to follow federal Social Security regulations. Illinois failed to commence welfare payments to Jordan (P), an eligible beneficiary, in the required time. Jordan (P) sued Edelman (D), the responsible official, to recover for the time he should have been receiving benefits. The district court issued an injunction compelling Edelman (D) to comply with the time guidelines and awarding "equitable restitution" in the amount Jordan (P) would have obtained had payments started in a timely fashion. The court of appeals affirmed. The Supreme Court granted review.

ISSUE: May a federal court fashion an equitable remedy compelling a state to make payments out of its treasury?

HOLDING AND DECISION: (Rehnquist, J.) No. A federal court cannot fashion an equitable remedy compelling a state to make payments out of its treasury. The sole exception to the Eleventh Amendment prohibition on federal actions where states are real parties in interest or defendants is when an action is brought under the Fourteenth Amendment or a statute thereunder. Even then, only prospective relief may be given; a state cannot be forced to make payments out of its treasury. Whether the relief is called "damages" or, as here, "equitable restitution" is irrelevant. A state cannot be compelled to make payments out of its treasury in a federal action, either in a legal or equitable action. Reversed.

DISSENT: (Douglas, J.) Where a state consents to participate in a federal program involving grants, it has waived its Eleventh Amendment immunities.

DISSENT: (Brennan, J.) The Eleventh Amendment does not bar federal suits against states by its own citizens.

DISSENT: (Marshall, J.) When a state voluntarily participates in a federal grant program, it waives its Eleventh Amendment protections, particularly where, as here, evidence of congressional intent that beneficiaries should have an avenue of redress exists.

EDITOR'S ANALYSIS: In terms of strict construction, the dissent of Justice Brennan is quite correct. The Eleventh Amendment, in its wording, does not bar federal suits against states by its own citizens. However, it is a by now well established rule that the Eleventh Amendment does apply to suits brought against states by its own citizens. Some have argued that such immunities are inherent in the American federal system, and the Eleventh Amendment merely reflects preexisting principles.

NOTES:

CHAPTER 5
PREVENTING HARM WITHOUT COERCION: DECLARATORY REMEDIES

QUICK REFERENCE RULES OF LAW

Adjudication of actual d/s in Fed. Ct

1. **Declaratory Judgments.** A court will decree specific performance of a personal property contract if the legal remedy is inadequate. (Nashville, Chattanooga, & St. Louis)

   Actual Case or Controversy

2. **Declaratory Judgments.** Courts may not refrain from deciding a counterclaim for declaratory judgment regarding the validity of a patent in infringement cases. (Cardinal Chemical Co. v. Morton International)

   not coercive, no irreparable injury showing needed

3. **Declaratory Judgments.** Federal declaratory relief may be given when threat of enforcement of a disputed state criminal statute exists. (Steffel v. Thompson)

4. **Declaratory Judgments.** A party cannot evade restrictions on federal injunctions against state criminal actions by joining parties not affected by the restrictions. (Doran v. Salem Inn)

5. **Quiet Title and the Like.** An action to quiet title to personalty may be brought. (Newman Machine Co. v. Newman)

6. **Reformation.** Reformation is allowed despite the lack of a mutual mistake if there is fraud by the other party. (Hand v. Dayton-Hudson)

NASHVILLE, CHATTANOOGA & ST. LOUIS RAILWAY
v. WALLACE
288 U.S. 249 (1933).

NATURE OF CASE: Appeal of declaratory relief action challenging state tax.

FACT SUMMARY: The Railway (P) sought a judicial declaration that a state gasoline tax was unconstitutional.

CONCISE RULE OF LAW: Federal courts may issue declaratory judgments when an actual controversy exists.

FACTS: Tennessee (D) instituted a gasoline storage tax. The Nashville, Chattanooga & St. Louis Railway (P) brought an action for a judicial declaration that the tax was an unconstitutional burden on interstate commerce. No additional legal or equitable relief was requested. The state trial court found the tax constitutional, and the state supreme court affirmed. The Railway (P) appealed to the U.S. Supreme Court.

ISSUE: May federal courts issue declaratory judgments when an actual controversy exists?

HOLDING AND DECISION: (Stone, J.) Yes. Federal courts may issue declaratory judgments when an actual controversy exists. Federal courts may decide cases or controversies, irrespective of the judicial labels given them. While declaratory relief may be in the form of an advisory opinion, it need not be, and the fact no relief other than the declaration is sought does not necessarily make an opinion merely advisory. Here, the respective rights of the parties are in controversy, and the holding of this Court will decide this controversy. Thus, jurisdiction is proper in this Court. (The Court went on to affirm.)

EDITOR'S ANALYSIS: Federal courts may only decide cases or controversies, per Article III, § 2 of the Constitution. Advisory opinions are not permitted; an adjudication of actual rights must be made. However, as the Court here points out, an adjudication of rights in and of itself may be all that a case requires.

NOTES:

CARDINAL CHEMICAL CO. v. MORTON INTERNATIONAL
113 S. Ct. 1967 (1993).

NATURE OF CASE: Appeal from vacation of declaratory judgment regarding patent validity.

FACT SUMMARY: The court of appeals refused to decide a counterclaim by Cardinal (D) seeking a declaration that Morton's (P) patent was invalid after Cardinal (D) prevailed in Morton's (P) infringement suit.

CONCISE RULE OF LAW: Courts may not refrain from deciding a counterclaim for declaratory judgment regarding the validity of a patent in infringement cases.

FACTS: Morton (P) owned two patents on chemical compounds used in polyvinyl chloride. In 1983, Morton (P) filed a suit alleging that Cardinal (D) had infringed those patents. Cardinal (D) counterclaimed for a declaratory judgment that the patents were invalid. The trial court found that Cardinal (D) had proved that the patents were invalid and gave two judgments in favor of Cardinal (D), dismissing the action for infringement and declaring the patents invalid. Morton (P) appealed, and the court of appeals vacated the declaration of invalidity on the basis of a rule that courts should refrain, on mootness grounds, from deciding the merits of a patent validity claim when infringement action is dismissed. Cardinal (D) appealed from this ruling.

ISSUE: May a court refrain from deciding a counterclaim for declaratory judgment regarding the validity of a patent where no infringement is proved?

HOLDING AND DECISION: (Stevens, J.) No. Courts may not refrain from deciding a counterclaim for declaratory judgment regarding the validity of a patent in patent infringement cases. A party seeking a declaratory judgment has the burden of establishing the existence of an actual case or controversy. In patent litigation, a party may satisfy that burden even if there is no infringement claim. Merely the desire to avoid the threat of an infringement action is sufficient to establish a controversy under the Declaratory Judgment Act. An actual charge of infringement necessarily indicates a controversy adequate to support jurisdiction. A counterclaim for declaratory judgment of invalidity is an independent claim that must be decided unless the other party proves that subsequent events have made the claim moot. Thus, a per se rule that validity declarations are vacated when the underlying infringement claim is dismissed is inappropriate. Furthermore, strong public policy concerns indicate that a counterclaim for declaratory judgment should be decided. Companies once charged with infringement will remain concerned about the risk of future charges if they develop similar products in the future. Also, relitigating the validity of patents is wasteful. The per se rule also deprives the patent holder of appellate review of the decision. Accordingly, the judgment of the court of appeals is reversed, and the case is remanded.

CONCURRENCE: (Scalia, J.) The majority decision seems to suggest that the court of appeals cannot decline review of patent validity judgments under any circumstances. However, only supposed mootness should be rejected as grounds for denying review.

EDITOR'S ANALYSIS: The decision noted that before the adoption of the Declaratory Judgment Act, patent holders often used "scarecrow patents." These patent holders would attempt to assert claims through settlements without ever actually filing suit. The alleged infringer was placed in a difficult position because he could not determine whether the patent was valid until the holder brought an infringement action.

NOTES:

THOMPSON v. COMMONWEALTH
197 Va. 208, 89 S.E.2d 64 (1955).

NATURE OF CASE: Appeal from decree of specific performance in action to enforce a contract.

FACT SUMMARY: Virginia (P) brought an action against Thompson (D) and his company to compel compliance with a contract to deliver spare parts for a vote counting system installed by Thompson (D).

CONCISE RULE OF LAW: A court will decree specific performance of a personal property contract if the legal remedy is inadequate.

FACTS: In 1945, Thompson (D) contracted with Virginia (P) to install certain vote counting apparatus in the state legislature and to furnish spare parts. Thompson (D) later reneged on supplying the spare parts, and Virginia (P) brought an action to compel compliance. Evidence showed the parts were not made by any other entity. The trial court decreed specific performance, and Thompson (D) appealed.

ISSUE: Will a court decree specific performance in a personal property contract if the legal remedy is inadequate?

HOLDING AND DECISION: (Smith, J.) Yes. A court will decree specific performance of a personal property contract if the legal remedy is inadequate. Generally contracts involving personal property are not subject to specific performance. This is merely because damages are usually adequate. Where damages are not adequate, specific performance will lie. Here, no other source of the needed spare parts appears to exist, so no alternate way of obtaining them can be found. This being the case, damages will not suffice. Affirmed.

EDITOR'S ANALYSIS: The defendants argued that to compel them to work on the contract was tantamount to involuntary servitude. The court did not buy that argument. As the court pointed out, the defendants had the option of subcontracting the necessary work.

NOTES:

STEFFEL v. THOMPSON
415 U.S. 452 (1974).

NATURE OF CASE: Appeal of denial of declaratory relief in civil rights action.

FACT SUMMARY: Steffel (P), prosecuted for trespassing while handing out leaflets, sought declaratory relief holding the law invalid.

CONCISE RULE OF LAW: Federal declaratory relief may be given when threat of enforcement of a disputed state criminal statute exists.

FACTS: Steffel (P) was threatened with prosecution under a criminal trespass law for handing out leaflets on private property. Steffel (P) then filed an action for injunctive and declaratory relief against the statute. The court of appeals denied both forms of relief, and Steffel (P) appealed only as to the declaratory relief. The state court had voluntarily stayed its proceedings pending the outcome of the federal action.

ISSUE: May federal declaratory relief be given when threat of enforcement of a disputed state criminal statute exists?

HOLDING AND DECISION: (Brennan, J.) Yes. Federal declaratory relief may be given when threat of enforcement of a disputed state criminal statute exists. Declaratory relief, unlike injunctive relief, is not coercive in that the threat of contempt does not exist. For that reason, the federalism concerns underlying the limitations on federal injunctions against pending state actions do not apply. Also, the traditional requisite of irreparable injury does not apply, so the problems of showing irreparable injury in an injunctive action of this nature does not apply in a declaratory relief action. Reversed.

CONCURRENCE: (Rehnquist, J.) It seems that Congress intended that seeking declaratory relief would be a preferable alternative to violating a law to test its constitutionality.

EDITOR'S ANALYSIS: Federal declaratory relief actions present certain problems. Ripeness is a big issue, as federal courts can only decide actual cases or controversies. Declaratory relief actions border on advisory opinions, which federal courts cannot do. However, as this case shows, federal declaratory relief actions are accepted as part of federal jurisprudence.

NOTES:

DORAN v. SALEM INN
422 U.S. 922 (1975).

NATURE OF CASE: Appeal of injunction prohibiting enforcement of ordinance proscribing topless dancing.

FACT SUMMARY: M&L Restaurant (P) obtained an injunction against enforcement of a criminal ordinance during the pendency of a prosecution under the ordinance.

CONCISE RULE OF LAW: A party cannot evade restrictions on federal injunctions against state criminal actions by joining parties not affected by the restrictions.

FACTS: The town of North Hempstead (D) passed an ordinance forbidding topless dancing. M&L Restaurant (P) and two other establishments filed suit to have the ordinance invalidated. M&L Restaurant (P), unlike the other establishments, continued to feature topless dancing. M&L (P) and its principals were served with criminal summonses. The district court found the ordinance unconstitutional and enjoined its enforcement. The district court held that federal restrictions on enjoining state criminal proceedings did not apply in M&L's (P) case, since M&L's (P) co-plaintiffs were entitled to relief. North Hempstead (D) appealed. The court of appeals affirmed.

ISSUE: Can a party evade restrictions on federal injunctions against state criminal actions by joining parties not affected by the restrictions?

HOLDING AND DECISION: (Rehnquist, J.) No. A party cannot evade restrictions on federal injunctions against state criminal actions by joining parties not affected by the restrictions. It is true that deciding the validity of a statute in a state criminal action and a federal action is not an efficient use of judicial manpower. However, as important as judicial economy may be, the federalism concerns in this area are greater. The states' rights considerations that lead to the rules regarding injunctions against pending state proceedings have full force even when the subject party is joined by non-affected parties, as is the case here. Reversed as to M&L (P).

EDITOR'S ANALYSIS: A sub-issue the Court dealt with was whether an injunction, as opposed to declaratory relief, was an appropriate remedy for the other plaintiffs. The court held that injunctive relief was proper, noting that the practical effect of the two was virtually identical. This is interesting, as the Court's holding in Steffel v. Thompson, 415 U.S. 452 (1974), was supposedly based on the differences between the two.

NOTES:

NEWMAN MACHINE CO. v. NEWMAN
275 N.C. 189, 166 S.E.2d 63 (1969).

NATURE OF CASE: Action to quiet title on personal property.

FACT SUMMARY: Newman (D) claimed he had been defrauded when he sold Newman Machine Co. (P) and demanded rescission.

CONCISE RULE OF LAW: An action to quiet title to personalty may be brought.

FACTS: Newman (D) owned certain shares in Newman Machine Co. (P), both individually and as trustee. Newman (D) sold a sizable number of shares to the corporation. Newman (D) later sought to rescind the transaction. Newman (D) and his attorneys continued to threaten legal action against Newman Machine Co. (P). Newman Machine Co. (P) then brought an action to quiet title as to the shares. Newman (D) demurred, claiming that North Carolina statues only provided for actions to quiet title to realty.

ISSUE: May an action to quiet title to personalty be brought?

HOLDING AND DECISION: (Huskins, J.) Yes. An action to quiet title to personalty may be brought. While statutory authorization exists only for quiet title actions in realty, suits in equity to quiet title existed before the statute. Where the usual elements necessary for an action in equity concur, no reason exists for not permitting personalty quiet title actions. Here, as Newman Machine Co. (P) is in possession, it cannot bring an action at law. Newman (D) has not sued, and the claims of Newman (D) impair the marketability of the stock. As legal remedies appear inadequate, a quiet title action is proper.

EDITOR'S ANALYSIS: The precursor to the quiet title action was the bill to remove cloud on title. This was an equitable action to test the validity of any instrument clouding a title. It did not actually pass on ownership itself. The quiet title action actually does declare ownership rights.

NOTES:

HAND v. DAYTON-HUDSON
775 F.2d 757 (6th Cir. 1985).

NATURE OF CASE: Appeal from order of reformation summary judgment dismissing an age discrimination and breach of contract action.

FACT SUMMARY: Hand (P), an attorney, altered a release that he and his employer, Dayton-Hudson (D), executed when Hand (P) was fired and accepted a payment.

CONCISE RULE OF LAW: Reformation is allowed despite the lack of a mutual mistake if there is fraud by the other party.

FACTS: Hand (P) was employed as an attorney at Dayton-Hudson (D) from 1967 to 1982. In 1982, Hand (P) was fired, and Dayton-Hudson (D) agreed to pay $38,000 if Hand (P) agreed to release Dayton-Hudson (D) from any claims. Hand (P) initially refused, but a release was drafted and presented to Hand (P). Hand (P) then prepared another release that was identical in form to the original release except that it provided that Hand (P) could bring an age discrimination and breach of contract claim. Hand (P) attached the release to the other documents in the same way as the original and tricked Dayton-Hudson (D) into signing the new release and paying the $38,000. Hand (P) then brought a suit for age discrimination and breach of contract against Dayton-Hudson (D), who sought reformation of the release and a dismissal of the discrimination suit. The trial court held that Hand (P) had committed fraud, reformed the release to conform to its original meaning, and dismissed Hand's (P) action. Hand (P) appealed.

ISSUE: Is reformation allowed despite the lack of a mutual mistake if there is fraud by the other party?

HOLDING AND DECISION: (Contie, J.) Yes. Reformation is allowed despite the lack of a mutual mistake if there is fraud by the other party. Although there is a general rule that a party is responsible for contracts that it has signed, it is not applicable where the signing is induced by fraud. Hand (P) committed fraud against Dayton-Hudson (D) by not informing them of the changes that he had purposefully made to the release. Generally, reformation of a contract is only available where there is a mutual mistake of fact. To grant reformation when there is a unilateral mistake would harm one party because the reformed contract would not represent what the parties intended. However, there is an exception to this rule where there is fraud or inequitable conduct by one party to the contract. If there is clear and convincing evidence that one party knew that the contract did not reflect the other party's intent, reformation may be allowed. A meeting of minds on the content of the reformed contract is not required because the exception is designed primarily to combat the inequities of fraud. Hand (P) was aware of Dayton-Hudson's

(D) intent regarding its original release and willfully acted to make Dayton-Hudson (D) believe that it was signing the original version. Thus, Hand's (P) conduct fits squarely within the exception, and reformation to conform to Dayton-Hudson's (D) understanding is allowed. Affirmed.

CONCURRENCE: (Wellford, J.) Reformation should not be allowed unless there has been a meeting of the minds on the substantive content of the reformed contract. However, Hand (P) should not be entitled to relitigate his discrimination claim because of his unconscionable conduct.

EDITOR'S ANALYSIS: This decision goes against the usual rule that reformation should be used to change a written contract to reflect the actual agreement of the parties. In Hand's (P) case, it doesn't appear that an agreement ever existed because Hand (P) would not have signed the release if it had not specifically exempted the discrimination and breach claims. If the release had been rescinded for fraud, Dayton-Hudson (D) would have recouped the $38,000 paid to Hand (P), who then would have been allowed to pursue any claims against the company.

NOTES:

6

CHAPTER 6
BENEFIT TO DEFENDANT AS THE MEASURE OF RELIEF: RESTITUTION

QUICK REFERENCE RULES OF LAW

Tortious wrongdoer
Restitution Principle

1. **The Basic Principle: Preventing Unjust Enrichment.** If the wrongdoer is consciously tortious in acquiring a benefit at the expense of the injured party, he is liable for what the injured party has lost and is deprived of any profit he may have gained. (Olwell v. Nye & Nissen Co.)

Infringement

2. **The Basic Principle: Preventing Unjust Enrichment.** In an infringement action under the Lanham Trademark Act, the plaintiff may, if successful, recover defendant's profits even if defendant was not in direct competition with, and therefore not diverting any trade from, plaintiff. (Maier Brewing Co. v. Fleishmann)

Fiduciary relationship + Constructive Trust

3. **The Basic Principle: Preventing Unjust Enrichment.** A constructive trust is a proper manner of disgorging the profits of one who abuses a confidential position. (Snepp v. United States)

Copyright infringement + restitution

4. **Apporting Profits.** A court may apportion profits in a suit for copyright infringement based upon the actual use of the copyrighted material in the production of the revenue. (Sheldon v. Metro-Goldwyn Pictures Corp.)

Trade secrets + I.P. usual remedy is restitution

5. **Apporting Profits.** Disgorgement of profits is a proper remedy for misappropriation of trade secrets. (USM Corp. v. Marson Fastener Corp.)

Insurance Co.

6. **Reversing Transactions: Rescission and the Like.** Insurers may avoid liability under any insurance policy where the applicant has made material misrepresentations as to his medical history. (Mutual Benefit Life Insurance Co. v. JMR Electronics Corp.)

Quasi - Contract   - (implied)

7. **Reversing Transactions: Rescission and the Like.** A party may recover for the expenditures made in reliance on the promise of another, even though the promisor received no benefit from such expenditures. (Farash v. Sykes Datatronics)

Rescission → as if K had not been made

8. **Tracing Defendant's Benefit: Restitution and Insolvency.** Equitable relief should be granted when damages will prove inadequate. (Hicks v. Clayton)

Constructive Trusts + no fraud

9. **Tracing Defendant's Benefit: Restitution and Insolvency.** Constructive trusts will not be given effect over federal bankruptcy proceedings unless actual fraud has occurred. (In re North Ameeerican Coin & Currency)

wrongfully obtained Commingled funds

10. **Tracing Defendant's Benefit: Restitution and Insolvency.** Wrongfully converted funds may be traced into commingled accounts without precise identification. (In re Erie Trust Co.)

Constructive trust is to equity (but restitution is at law)

11. **Tracing Defendant's Benefit: Restitution and Insolvency.** A constructive trust arises when a person holding title to property is subject to an equitable duty to convey it to another on the ground that he would be unjustly enriched if he were permitted to retain it. (Rogers v. Rogers)

Improvements on property - equitable lien

12. **Tracing Defendant's Benefit: Restitution and Insolvency.** One permitting another to make improvements on his property is liable for the value thereof. (Robinson v. Robinson)

subrogation - insurer sues after 3rd party

13. **Other Restitutionary Remedies — Subrogation, Indemnity, and Contribution.** An agent who buys stock from a principal due to the negligence of a third party has standing to sue the third party. (American National Bank & Trust v. Weyerhaeuser Co.)

Appreciated value of returned property

14. **Other Restitutionary Remedies — Actions to Recover Specific Property: Replevin, Ejectment, and the Like.** Rightful owners may recover both converted property and its estimated appreciated value if subsequent alterations have damaged the property. (Welch v. Kosasky)

OLWELL v. NYE & NISSEN CO.

Wash. Sup. Ct., 26 Wash.2d 282, 173 P.2d 652, 169 A.L.R. 139 (1946).

NATURE OF CASE: Action for damages for unjust enrichment.

FACT SUMMARY: Nye (D) used Olwell's (P) egg washing machine without the owner's permission or knowledge in order to make up for a manpower shortage during World War II.

CONCISE RULE OF LAW: If the wrongdoer is consciously tortious in acquiring a benefit at the expense of the injured party, he is liable for what the injured party has lost and is deprived of any profit he may have gained.

FACTS: Olwell (P) sold and transferred his one-half interest in an egg packing company to Nye (D) with Olwell (P) to retain full ownership of an egg washing machine formerly used by the packing company. Olwell (P) arranged to have the machine stored in space adjacent to Nye (D) but not covered by its lease. After the start of World War II, there was a manpower shortage, and Nye's (D) treasurer ordered that the egg washer be taken out of storage and put into operation. This was done without Olwell's (P) knowledge or permission in May, 1941. The machine was used once a week until Olwell learned of it in about January, 1945. Olwell (P) offered to sell Nye (D) the machine for $600, half its 1929 cost, but Nye's (D) counteroffer of $50 was refused. Olwell (P) then sought to recover $25 a month and was awarded $10 per week, or $1,560.

ISSUE: Where a wrongdoer is consciously tortious in acquiring a benefit at the expense of the injured party, may such party recover not only his actual losses but the tortfeasor's profits as well?

HOLDING AND DECISION: (Mallery, J.) Yes. Where a defendant tortfeasor has benefitted by his wrong, the plaintiff can waive the tort and bring an action in assumpsit for restitution. Nye's (D) saving of labor costs was a recoverable benefit. It is no defense that Olwell (P) was just as well off whether or not the machine was used. There is no benefit to property ownership unless the owner has a right to exclusive use. Where a defendant has tortiously received a benefit, he must pay for what the other has lost although it is more than the benefit. If he was consciously tortious, he must be deprived of any profit he derived from subsequent use as well.

EDITOR'S ANALYSIS: Notice that the measure of damages in cases of misuse of another's property depends on the willfulness of the defendant's conduct. Where he consciously misuses another's property, he pays for the owner's loss and loses any profit he may have made. But it he is no more at fault than the plaintiff, he need not pay for losses in excess of his benefit, and he may retain his profit. Note that the damages were reduced only because the amount awarded was greater than Olwell's (P) prayer. Note also that had Olwell used an assumpsit theory of implied sale of the egg washer to Nye (D), he would probably have recovered even less as the machine's inherent value was most likely much less than the amount its use saved Nye (D).

NOTES:

MAIER BREWING CO. v. FLEISCHMANN DISTILLING CORP.
390 F.2d 117 (9th Cir. 1968),
cert. den. 391 U.S. 966

NATURE OF CASE: Action for an accounting and injunction under the Lanham Trademark Act.

FACT SUMMARY: Maier Brewing (D) marketed "Black & White" beer, thereby infringing on the registered trademark of Fleischmann's (P) whiskey.

CONCISE RULE OF LAW: In an infringement action under the Lanham Trademark Act, the plaintiff may, if successful, recover defendant's profits even if defendant was not in direct competition with, and therefore not diverting any trade from, plaintiff.

FACTS: Fleischmann's (P) "Black & White" trademark for its Scotch whiskey was registered with the patent office. Maier Brewing (D) introduced onto the market a beer labelled "Black & White." In an action under the Lanham Act, the trial court ordered an injunction and an accounting not only against Maier Brewing (D), but also against Ralph's Grocery (D) which carried the beer.

ISSUE: In order for a plaintiff to seek an accounting under the Lanham Act, must he prove diversion on trade?

HOLDING AND DECISION: (Byrne, J.) No. The majority view regards an accounting of profits by the defendant as a method of shifting the burden of proof as to damages for lost or potentially lost sales from the plaintiff to the defendant. This view requires that there be competition between the parties before this recovery can be granted. The more recent trend, adopted here, is based on the equitable concepts of restitution and unjust enrichment. If Maier Brewing (D) has used Fleischmann's (P) registered trademark for its own profit, it should account for taking this property interest. Fleischmann (P) is entitled, furthermore, to protection of its good will, and the public is entitled to protection against falsely marketed goods. To mitigate the apparent harshness of this rule, which seeks to make trademark infringements unprofitable, Fleischmann (P) is not entitled to profits demonstrably not attributable to the unlawful use of the mark.

EDITOR'S ANALYSIS: Apart from an accounting, the plaintiff in a Lanham Act suit is entitled to recover any actual damages sustained, his court costs, trebled damages in cases of bad-faith infringement, or where he is unable to prove any personal losses or any profits to the defendant, a compensatory "in lieu" award of damages.

SNEPP v. UNITED STATES
444 U.S. 507 (1980).

NATURE OF CASE: Appeal of reversal of order declaring constructive trust.

FACT SUMMARY: Reneging on a preemployment agreement ex-CIA agent Snepp (D) published a book about his experience without obtaining prepublication clearance.

CONCISE RULE OF LAW: A constructive trust is a proper manner of disgorging the profits of one who abuses a confidential position.

FACTS: Snepp (D), prior to becoming a CIA agent, signed an agreement that he would not publish classified information, and that he would submit any materials he intended to publish for agency review. After leaving the agency, Snepp (P) published a book of his experiences without prepublication review. The book contained no classified information. The Government (P) brought an action to enjoin further breaches of the agreement and to compel Snepp (P) to turn over profits from the book. The district court granted the requested relief, issuing an injunction and ordering a constructive trust. The court of appeals reversed the constructive trust, holding that Snepp (D) had a right to publish nonclassified information.

ISSUE: Is a constructive trust a proper manner of disgorging the profits of one who abused a confidential position?

HOLDING AND DECISION: (Per Curiam) Yes. A constructive trust is a proper manner of disgorging the profits of one who abuses a confidential position. Where one abuses a position of trust to the detriment of the one placing the abuser in the position of trust, any profits derived therefrom rightfully belong to the trustor. The imposition of a constructive trust is the proper way for the abuse to be corrected. Here, Snepp (D) was in a position of trust and he abused it, by violating an express promise to allow prepublication review of his materials. In so doing he has possibly compromised the Government's (P) position in sensitive areas, and he should not profit from this. Reversed.

DISSENT: (Stevens, J.) The only legitimate purpose of the agreement would have been the prevention of publication of classified information, something that did not occur. Consequently, the Government (P) was not injured.

EDITOR'S ANALYSIS: The constructive trust has become a very common remedy for unjust enrichment. It developed in instances where a fiduciary relationship was abused as in the present case. It has, however, also been applied to situations where no such relationship ever existed.

SHELDON v. METRO-GOLDWYN PICTURES CORP.
309 U.S. 390 (1940).

NATURE OF CASE: Appeal from an award of damages for copyright infringement.

FACT SUMMARY: Sheldon (P) contended he should receive all of Metro-Goldwyn's (D) net profits for the latter's motion picture which was found to infringe upon Sheldon's (P) copyrighted play.

CONCISE RULE OF LAW: A court may apportion profits in a suit for copyright infringement based upon the actual use of the copyrighted material in the production of the revenue.

FACTS: Sheldon (P) sued Metro-Goldwyn (D), contending the latter's motion picture infringed on Sheldon's (P) copyrighted play. The trial court adopted the findings of a special master and awarded Sheldon (P) all of Metro's (D) net profit from the movie. The court of appeals modified the award, granting recovery equal to one-fifth of the total. This was done in recognition of the fact that the play itself did not account for 100% of the films' profits. Sheldon (P) appealed.

ISSUE: May a court apportion damages in a copyright infringement suit?

HOLDING AND DECISION: (Hughes, C.J.) Yes. A court may apportion profits in a suit for copyright infringement based upon the actual use of the copyrighted material in the production of the revenue. There are many factors inherent in a motion picture which make it more profitable than a play using the same raw material. The drawing power of the stars, the skill of the director, and the accessibility of the performance are things clearly unrelated to the use of the play. Thus, an apportionment of the profits was necessary for a just result. Affirmed.

EDITOR'S ANALYSIS: The Court could not articulate a concrete standard to be used in apportionment cases. It compared the compensation paid other screenwriters for their work, yet some were compensated in a lump sum while others received a percentage of the gross or net receipts. Adding to the difficulty was the problem of determining how much of the play was plagiarized. It is clearly an area of commercial activity which does not lend itself to precise calculation.

NOTES:

USM CORP. v. MARSON FASTENER CORP.
Mass. Sup. Ct. 467 N.E. 2d 1271 (1984).

NATURE OF CASE: Appeal from judgment awarding damages for misappropriation of trade secrets.

FACT SUMMARY: A trial court awarded USM Corp. (P) damages against Marson Fastener (D) for trade secret infringement in an amount equal to Marson's (D) profits.

CONCISE RULE OF LAW: Disgorgement of profits is a proper remedy for misappropriation of trade secrets.

FACTS: Marson Fastener Corp. (D) lured Lahnston (D), an engineer, away from USM Corp. (P) Using trade secrets belonging to USM (P), Marson (D) was able to improve a type of rivet it manufactured, which had heretofore not sold well. From 1965 to 1980, Marson (D) profited from selling the improved rivet. USM Corp. (P) sued Masson (D) for misappropriation of trade secrets. A jury found that misappropriation had occurred. The court awarded damages based on Marson's (D) profits attributable to the misappropriation. Marson (D) appealed.

ISSUE: Is disgorgement of profits a proper remedy for misappropriation of trade secrets?

HOLDING AND DECISION: (Wilkins, J.) Yes. Disgorgement of profits is a proper remedy for misappropriation of trade secrets. The guiding principle in such a case is to order the wrongdoing defendant to give up all gain attributable to the misuse of the trade secret and to measure that gain as accurately as possible. Disgorgement of profits is the best measure of damages for achieving that goal, even if the aggrieved plaintiff's demonstrable damages are significantly less. [The court went on to discuss the mechanics of applying the measure of damages. A court initially looks at the gross profits realized by sales of the offending product, and this is the presumptive amount of damages. The burden is on the defendant to prove offsets based on expenses incurred in marketing the product. The court also held prejudgment interest to be available, as well as punitive damages.] Affirmed.

EDITOR'S ANALYSIS: The measure of damages used here is called "restitution." Restitution looks not to the aggrieved party's losses but rather to the culpable party's ill-gotten gain. Often restitutionary damages will have little relation to a plaintiff's actual out-of-pocket loss. Nonetheless, restitution is the usual measure of damages in intellectual property cases.

NOTES:

**MUTUAL BENEFIT LIFE INSURANCE CO. v. JMR
ELECTRONICS CORP.**
848 F.2d 30 (2d Cir. 1988).

NATURE OF CASE: Appeal from a judgment ordering rescission of an insurance policy.

FACT SUMMARY: After Gaon, the president of JMR (D), falsely answered questions on an insurance application regarding his smoking, Mutual Benefit (P) sought to rescind the policy.

CONCISE RULE OF LAW: Insurers may avoid liability under any insurance policy where the applicant has made material misrepresentations as to his medical history.

FACTS: In 1985, JMR (D) submitted an application to Mutual Benefit (P) for a $250,000 insurance policy on the life of its president, Gaon. Since Gaon answered questions on the application indicating that he was a nonsmoker, Mutual (P) issued a policy at the nonsmoker premium rate. In 1986, Gaon died. During a routine investigation of JMR's (D) claim, Mutual (P) discovered that Gaon had actually smoked half a pack of cigarettes a day for a continuous period of ten years. Mutual (P) then brought an action seeking a declaration that the policy was void. The trial court granted summary judgment to Mutual (P) and ordered rescission of the insurance contract, which included the return of JMR's (D) premiums. JMR (D) appealed, arguing that the misrepresentation was not material because Mutual (P) would have provided insurance — albeit at a higher rate — even if Gaon had disclosed his smoking habit.

ISSUE: May insurers avoid liability under any insurance policy where the applicant has made material misrepresentations as to his medical history?

HOLDING AND DECISION: (Per curiam) Yes. Insurers may avoid liability under any insurance policy where the applicant has made any material misrepresentations as to his medical history. Under New York law, even an innocent misrepresentation as to the applicant's medical history is sufficient to allow the insurer to rescind the policy if the misrepresentation is material. A false statement is material if knowledge by the insurer of the true facts would lead to a refusal by the insurer to issue the contract or if the insurer is induced to accept an application it might have otherwise refused. The materiality inquiry is made with respect to the particular policy issued in reliance on the misrepresentation. Clearly, Mutual (P) was induced to issue the nonsmoker discounted policy to JMR (D) as a result of the false statements made by Gaon on the application. Even though Mutual (P) may have issued a policy to JMR (D) at a higher premium if it had been aware of the true facts, an insurer is allowed to rescind a particular policy if there were material misrepresentations on the application. A contrary result would encourage the

misrepresentation of facts by applicants since they could be assured that, if the claims were contested, they would still be entitled to coverage of some type. Affirmed.

EDITOR'S ANALYSIS: Rescission cancels the transaction and seeks to place each party in the position he occupied prior to the contract. Thus, in the instant case, JMR (D) was entitled to the return of all the premiums it had paid to Mutual Benefit (P), with interest. Mutual (P) was released of all obligations. Rescission is also available for fraud, mutual mistake, and duress.

NOTES:

FARASH v. SYKES DATATRONICS, INC.

N.Y. Ct. of App., 59 N.Y.2d 500, 465 N.Y.S.2d 917, 452 N.E.2d 1245 (1983).

NATURE OF CASE: Appeal from dismissal of action for quantum meruit.

FACT SUMMARY: Farash (P) sued to recover expenditures for remodeling his building made in reliance on Sykes's (D) oral agreement to lease.

CONCISE RULE OF LAW: A party may recover for the expenditures made in reliance on the promise of another, even though the promisor received no benefit from such expenditures.

FACTS: Farash (P) and Sykes (D) entered into an oral agreement whereby Sykes (D) would lease Farash's (P) building, and Farash (P) would remodel it to fit Sykes' (D) needs. Sykes (D) subsequently refused to lease the building. Farash (P) sued, contending that although the lease was unenforceable under the Statute of Frauds, he was entitled to recover the expenses incurred in remodeling the building in reliance on Sykes' (D) promise to lease it. The trial court denied Sykes' (D) motion to dismiss, but the appellate court reversed on the basis that Sykes (D) was not benefited by the expenditures.

ISSUE: May a party recover for expenditures made in reliance on the promise of another even though the promisor received no benefit from the expenditures?

HOLDING AND DECISION: (Cooke, C.J.) Yes. A party may recover the expenditures made in reliance on the promise of another even though the promisor received no benefit from such expenditures. In order to recover in quasi-contract, the plaintiff need not show that the defendant physically received benefits from the performance. It is sufficient that such performance was part of an agreed-upon exchange; it is deemed received by the defendant. As a result, Farash (P) did state a cause of action. Reversed.

DISSENT: (Jasen, J.) In order to recover in quasi-contract, the plaintiff must demonstrate that the defendant was unjustly enriched by his actions.

EDITOR'S ANALYSIS: Quasi-contract is one of the common counts and is an action to enforce a contract which is implied in law. The basis for recovery is to prevent the defendant from benefiting unjustly from the plaintiff's performance. Some commentators argue that the implied receipt concept relied upon in this case is an artificial label when used in the context of unjust enrichment.

HICKS v. CLAYTON

Cal. Ct. of App., 67 Cal.App.3d 251, 136 Cal.Rptr. 512 (1977).

NATURE OF CASE: Appeal of award of damages for fraud.

FACT SUMMARY: Clayton (D), Hicks' (P) attorney, swindled Hicks (P) out of real property in exchange for worthless negotiable instruments.

CONCISE RULE OF LAW: Equitable relief should be granted when damages will prove inadequate.

FACTS: Clayton (D) was Hicks' (P) lawyer. Clayton (D) received certain real property in exchange for worthless stocks and notes. Clayton (D) failed to pay on the notes, and Hicks (P) was unable to pay off his own loan on the property, which remained. A tax lien was also placed on the property. Hicks (P) sued for rescission and restitution. The court awarded Hicks (P) damages. Clayton (D) was insolvent at this time. Hicks (P) appealed.

ISSUE: Should equitable relief be granted when damages will prove inadequate?

HOLDING AND DECISION: (Staniforth, J.) Yes. Equitable relief should be granted when damages will prove inadequate. While the propriety of equitable relief is a matter of discretion, the discretion is not absolute. Where it appears damages will not compensate a plaintiff, the court has a duty to award appropriate equitable relief. Here, Clayton (D) was insolvent, and the property had a tax lien. Very little chance of Hicks (P) ever collecting damages exists. For this reason, rescission of the conveyance is the proper remedy. Reversed.

EDITOR'S ANALYSIS: Whether damages or rescission is awarded can make a vast difference in the collectability of a judgment. As an example, in the present action, had damages been awarded, Hicks (P) would have had to stand behind other creditors of Clayton (D). With rescission, the creditors of Clayton (D) have no claim on the property.

NOTES:

IN RE NORTH AMERICAN COIN & CURRENCY
767 F.2d 1573 (9th Cir. 1985).

NATURE OF CASE: Appeal from an order denying a constructive trust in a bankruptcy proceeding.

FACT SUMMARY: Customers (P) of North American Coin (NAC) (D) who had placed their orders after the principals of NAC (D) were aware of financial problems sought to have their money returned separate from the subsequent bankruptcy proceedings.

CONCISE RULE OF LAW: Constructive trusts will not be given effect over federal bankruptcy proceedings unless actual fraud has occurred.

FACTS: In 1982, NAC (D), a precious metals retailer, suffered severe financial losses. The persons who were responsible for the daily operation of NAC (D) met to solve the problem on September 12, 1982. They decided that they would attempt to keep the company afloat until a director and stockholder meeting the following week, when they hoped to receive new capital for NAC (D). They also created a bank account, labeled "Special Trust Account," into which they placed all the moneys they received from orders during the week of September 13–17. The purpose of this account was to protect new customers in case NAC (D) collapsed. Customers (P) of NAC (D) placed $600,000 in orders, which were deposited in the trust account before NAC (D) filed for bankruptcy. The customers (P) asserted that the bankruptcy trustee should hold those funds in the special account in constructive trust for them. The bankruptcy court rejected this argument and held that the customers (P) were merely creditors who must pursue their claims in the same manner as the other creditors. The customers (P) appealed.

ISSUE: May constructive trusts be given effect over federal bankruptcy proceedings

HOLDING AND DECISION: (Canby, J.) No. Constructive trusts will not be given effect over federal bankruptcy proceedings unless there has been actual fraud. A constructive trust is a remedy that is fashioned in equity to provide relief where a balancing of interests seems necessary. Arizona provides for the imposition of a constructive trust whenever title to property has been obtained through actual fraud or other means which render it unconscionable for the holder to retain title. A federal bankruptcy estate is not automatically deprived of any funds that a state law might find subject to a constructive trust. However, bankruptcy trustees do not have any interest in property that is acquired by fraud against the rightful owners. Actual fraud is characterized by a willful intent to deceive. If a debtor believes in good faith that a transaction will be carried out, there is no deceptive intent. In the present case, NAC (D) did not commit any fraudulent acts against the customers (P) since there is no evidence that NAC (D) had an intent to defraud. The principals of the company believed that the operation would continue and did not know that NAC (D) was insolvent when the special trust account was formed. The creation of the fund does not demonstrate a belief that NAC (D) could not meet its obligations but was merely a good-faith attempt to segregate the customers' (P) payments in the event that their orders could be completed. Therefore, there was no actual fraud, and the customers (P) do not have the right to impose a constructive trust on the moneys in the trust account. Affirmed.

EDITOR'S ANALYSIS: The decision also noted that the result was also fair to other customers of NAC (D) who lost money on orders that were not completed. The court reasoned that customers who placed orders prior to September 13 should have the same general creditor rights as those who happened to order a day later. Since constructive trusts are based on equitable principles, the trust was denied because there was no equitable basis on which to distinguish the customers (P) who brought suit.

NOTES:

IN RE ERIE TRUST CO.
Pa. Sup. Ct., 326 Pa. 198, 191 A. 613 (1937).

NATURE OF CASE: Appeal of adjudication determining possession of funds.

FACT SUMMARY: Erie Trust Co., before bankruptcy, converted funds from Gingrich, to which Gingrich's beneficiaries laid claim.

CONCISE RULE OF LAW: Wrongfully converted funds may be traced into commingled accounts without precise identification.

FACTS: Erie Trust Co. converted certain funds belonging to Gingrich. Upon Gingrich's death, a receiver attempted to recover the funds from the estate of Erie, which had gone bankrupt. Finding that the funds had been commingled in various deposit accounts and that the receiver could not trace which specific funds went to which specific account, the trial court refused to give the receiver preference over general creditors. The receiver appealed.

ISSUE: May wrongfully converted funds be traced into commingled accounts without precise identification?

HOLDING AND DECISION: (Stern, J.) Yes. Wrongfully converted funds may be traced into commingled accounts without precise identification. Given the complexities of modern banking, the burden of precise identification of funds in commingled accounts would be virtually impossible to meet. It is sufficient that the accounts into which the funds have been deposited be identified. Once this is done, the presumption arises that all withdrawals are of other funds, and the converted funds remain in the various accounts. This is the presumption that should have been applied here. Reversed.

EDITOR'S ANALYSIS: The basic rule in bankruptcy is that, after the government gets its share, senior creditors get priority. An exception exists where, as here, defrauded parties can prove which funds were theirs. In this instance, the law presumes that the bankrupt never had the property. The victims thereby leapfrog over the general creditors.

NOTES:

ROGERS v. ROGERS

N.Y. Ct. of App., 63 N.Y.2d 502, 483 N.Y.S.2d 976, 473 N.E.2d 226 (1984).

NATURE OF CASE: Appeal from dismissal of action for imposition of constructive trust.

FACT SUMMARY: The first wife of a man who agreed to maintain a $15,000 life insurance policy for the benefit of their children sued the man's second wife for the proceeds when they were paid to her on his death.

CONCISE RULE OF LAW: A constructive trust arises when a person holding title to property is subject to an equitable duty to convey it to another on the ground that he would be unjustly enriched if he were permitted to retain it.

FACTS: In a separation agreement, Jerome Rogers promised his first wife, Susan Rogers (P), to maintain in force a $15,000 life insurance policy for her benefit and the benefit of their children. During their marriage and for some time thereafter, Jerome worked for Grumman Aerospace and had a $15,000 policy through Travelers Insurance. Jerome, however, left Grumman and for six years had no life insurance. During this six-year period he also married Judith Rogers (D). Then Jerome got a job with Technical Data and received another $15,000 policy, issued through Phoenix Mutual. Four years later Jerome died, and Phoenix paid the $15,000 proceeds to Judith Rogers (D). Susan Rogers (P) sued Judith Rogers (D) to impress a constructive trust on the insurance proceeds for her own benefit and the benefit of her children. The trial court dismissed Susan's (P) complaint on the ground that the separation agreement did not address Jerome's duties in the event of cancellation or lapse of the policy issued through Travelers. Susan Rogers (P) appealed.

ISSUE: Does a constructive trust arise when a person holding title to property becomes subject to an equitable duty to convey it to another on the ground that he would be unjustly enriched if he were permitted to retain it?

HOLDING AND DECISION: (Kaye, J.) Yes. A constructive trust arises when a person holding title to property is subject to an equitable duty to convey it to another on the ground that he would be unjustly enriched if he were permitted to retain it. A promise in a separation agreement to maintain an insurance policy designating a spouse as beneficiary vests in the spouse an equitable interest in the policy specified, and that spouse will prevail over a person in whose favor the decedent executed a gratuitous change in beneficiary. Nor will the first spouse's superior right to the insurance proceeds be defeated simply because the insured changes policies or insurance companies instead of beneficiaries. Here, Jerome Rogers promised to maintain a $15,000 insurance policy for the benefit of Susan Rogers (P) and their children; this promise was not limited to his length of employ at Grumman and was not eviscerated by the

period between the lapse of his Travelers policy and his Phoenix policy issued during his employ at Technical data. Jerome Roger's obtaining of a $15,000 policy at Technical Data was merely a fulfillment of his implied promise to Susan Rogers (P) to replace the former Travelers policy. Therefore, a constructive trust is imposed on the Phoenix proceeds paid to Judith Rogers (D), and she is ordered to transfer them to Susan (P). Reversed.

EDITOR'S ANALYSIS: It is important to remember that constructive trusts are "equity's remedy" when one party is unjustly enriched at the expense of another, and is parallel to the implied contract or quantum meruit remedy available at law. It is also important to remember that a constructive trust differs greatly from an express trust, which arises because of a manifestation of an intention to create it and which gives rise to a fiduciary relationship. See Restatement of Restitution § 160. Constructive trusts come into existence only on the date of a court order. See Palmland Villas I Condominium v. Taylor, 390 So.2d 123 (Fla. App. 1980).

NOTES:

ROBINSON v. ROBINSON

Ill. Ct. App., 100 Ill.App.3d 437, 429 N.E.2d 183 (1981).

NATURE OF CASE: Appeal of court-imposed equitable lien on real property.

FACT SUMMARY: Ann Robinson (P), divorcing Wylie Robinson (D), asserted rights in property belonging to Wylie's (D) parents, Earl (D) and Alice (D), on which Ann (P) and Wylie (D) had made improvements.

CONCISE RULE OF LAW: One permitting another to make improvements on his property is liable for the value thereof.

FACTS: Ann (P) and Wylie (D) Robinson constructed a house on farm property belonging to Earl (D) and Alice (D) Robinson, Wylie's (D) parents. No express agreement that they would be given the property existed, but the parties treated the house as theirs. Ann (P) sued Wylie (D) for divorce, and claimed a one-half interest in the house. The trial court held that Ann (P) was entitled to one-half of the amount the improvements had increased the property value, charging the property with an equitable lien. Earl (D) and Alice (D) appealed.

ISSUE: Is one permitting another to make improvements on his property liable for the value thereof?

HOLDING AND DECISION: (Unverzagt, J.) Yes. One permitting another to make improvements on his property is liable for the value thereof. To allow one who stands by and allows another to improve his property without compensation is unjust. There will always be some element of fraud in such a situation, for no one will rationally improve another's property without expecting something in return, and the owner should realize this. Here, Alice (D) and Earl (D) must have known the younger Robinsons expected something in return, and by allowing the improvements they impliedly consented. (Partially reversed on other grounds.)

EDITOR'S ANALYSIS: The remedy chosen here was an equitable lien. This equitable remedy is similar in operation to a constructive trust. In a constructive trust the trustee is expected to return the entire res; in an equitable lien, the individual charged retains an interest in the res.

NOTES:

AMERICAN NATIONAL BANK & TRUST CO. v. WEYERHAEUSER CO.

692 F.2d 455 (7th Cir. 1982).

NATURE OF CASE: Appeal of dismissal of subrogation action.

FACT SUMMARY: A potential stock sale by the principal of American National (P) was lost due to the possible negligence of Weyerhaeuser (D), prompting American (P) to buy the stock.

CONCISE RULE OF LAW: An agent who buys stock from a principal due to the negligence of a third party has standing to sue the third party.

FACTS: American National (P) held 40,000 shares of Weyerhaeuser (D) stock for an investor. Weyerhaeuser (D) offered to buy the shares, and the investor instructed American National (P) to sell them. Due to a clerical error either by American National (P) or by Weyerhaeuser (D) or its agent the sale was never consummated. American National, to fulfill its contract, bought the shares, which it resold at a loss. American National (P) brought suit against Weyerhaeuser (D) for what it lost. The district court held that American National (P) did not have standing as it was not a real party in interest and granted summary judgment. American National (P) appealed.

ISSUE: Does an agent who buys stock from a principal due to the negligence of a third party have standing to sue the third party?

HOLDING AND DECISION: (Cudahy, J.) Yes. An agent who buys stock from a principal due to the negligence of a third party has standing to sue the third party. The principle of subrogation, if the requirements are met, allows one using his property to discharge the obligation of another to seek reimbursement against one otherwise unjustly enriched. First, the claim must be paid in full. American (P) did this, buying all stock tendered by the investor. Second, the subrogee must pay a claim for which a third party is primarily liable. In this case, an issue exists as to who was at fault; this must be resolved at trial. Third, the subrogor must have a right assertable against the third party. Here, if Weyerhaeuser (D) or its agent was negligent, the investor would have had a claim against either if American (P) had not bought the stock. Finally, the subrogee must have had a legal duty to have indemnified. Here, American (P) had a duty to sell the stock on behalf of the investor; had it failed to do so, it would have been in breach of contract. Therefore, since all the elements of subrogation existed or were disputed, summary judgment was improper. Reversed.

EDITOR'S ANALYSIS: Subrogation is an equitable procedure allowing one who indemnifies another to proceed against another when normally it would be an outsider to the relevant transaction.

The classical subrogation action involves insurance. When an insurer pays damages to an insured, subrogation gives the insurer the right to proceed directly against the party who damaged the insured.

NOTES:

① Claim paid in full

② Subrogee (insurer) pays for damage 3rd party did

③ Injured must have claim against 3rd party

④ Injured had legal duty to be indemnified.

WELCH v. KOSASKY
509 N.E.2d 919 (Mass. App. 1987).

NATURE OF CASE: Appeal of an award of damages for conversion.

FACT SUMMARY: Welch (P) sought to recover the appreciated value of antique silver stolen from her home, which Kosasky (D) had bought and then sold to other parties.

CONCISE RULE OF LAW: Rightful owners may recover both converted property and its estimated appreciated value if subsequent alterations have damaged the property.

FACTS: In 1974, twelve lots of antique silver were stolen from Welch's (P) home. A month later, Kosasky (D), who knew or should have known that the silver was stolen, bought eleven of the lots for $2,750. The items had been purchased by Welch (P) for over $40,000 before the theft. In 1981, Kosasky (D) sold the silver to a dealer. Shortly thereafter, Welch (P) saw some of the stolen items and eventually recovered all of the silver that Kosasky (D) had bought. Among the items were two James II castors, which had been altered by Kosasky (D). Welch (P) sued Kosasky (D) for conversion, and the trial court awarded $10,000 for the loss of use of the silver, $22,000 for diminution in the value of the James II castors, and $5,000 in consequential damages. Kosasky (D) appealed, contending that the trial court erred regarding damages for the James II castors because they had been bought in 1974 for only $7,500.

ISSUE: May rightful owners recover both converted property and its estimated appreciated value if subsequent alterations have damaged the property?

HOLDING AND DECISION: (Armstrong, J.) Yes. Rightful owners may recover both converted property and its estimated appreciated value if subsequent alterations have damaged the property. Generally, where the rightful owner elects to receive back goods that have been converted, replevin damages are measured by loss of use and the value of the converted goods at the time of the conversion. However, the converter is credited with the value of the returned goods at the time of the return. But there is no rule that the rightful owner is precluded from recovering the value of the converted property as appreciated, if an independent basis for the appreciation exists. Welch (P) had a legal right to the return of the James II castors, which would have had a value of $25,000 in 1981. However, since Kosasky (D) had altered the castors, they were only worth $3,000. This unauthorized alteration would have constituted trespass had Kosasky (D) been rightfully in possession. Therefore, replevin should allow Welch (P) to seek damages for both torts, the conversion and the trespass. Accordingly, the trial court was correct in awarding $22,000 to Welch (P) for the difference in the estimated appreciated value of the castors and their current value at the time of return. Affirmed.

EDITOR'S ANALYSIS: Technically, the suit in the Welch (P) case was not replevin because Welch (P) had already recovered her silver. However, the remedies available are identical. The most common use of replevin is to compel the return of personal property, and it may be invoked in situations involving theft, conversion, or repossession of collateral.

NOTES:

CHAPTER 7
PUNITIVE REMEDIES

QUICK REFERENCE RULES OF LAW

Corporations

1. **Punitive Damages — Common Law and Statutes.** A corporate decision to expose the public to serious danger when inexpensive alternatives exist is a legitimate basis for punitive damages. (Grimshaw v. Ford Motor Co.)

2. **Punitive Damages — The Constitution.** In determining whether a particular award is so grossly excessive as to violate the Due Process Clause, a general rule of reasonableness must be followed. (TXO Production Corp. v. Alliance Resources Corp.)

3. **Punitive Damages in Contract.** Plaintiffs may only receive punitive damages for breach of an implied covenant if there is at least one finding of an independent tort with accompanying actual damages. (Transcontinental Gas Pipe Line Corp. v. American National Petroleum Co.)

GRIMSHAW v. FORD MOTOR CO.

Cal. Ct. App., 119 Cal.App.3d 757 (1981).

NATURE OF CASE: Appeal of award of punitive damages for products liability.

FACT SUMMARY: Ford Motor Co. (D) marketed the Pinto with knowledge of excessive vulnerability of the fuel tank.

CONCISE RULE OF LAW: A corporate decision to expose the public to serious danger when inexpensive alternatives exist is a legitimate basis for punitive damages.

FACTS: Ford Motor Co. (D) marketed the Pinto, a vehicle conceived to be small and inexpensive. Concern about the vulnerability of the fuel tank was expressed to management. Despite the fact that the tank could be given greater protection relatively inexpensively, management believed such improvements were not cost-effective. In 1972, a Pinto carrying Grimshaw (P) was hit from behind, bursting into flames. Gray, the driver, was killed, and Grimshaw (P) was burned. A jury returned a verdict which included $125,000,000 in punitive damages, which the court remitted to $3,500,000. Ford (D) appealed.

ISSUE: Is a corporate decision to expose the public to serious danger when inexpensive alternatives exist a legitimate basis for punitive damages?

HOLDING AND DECISION: (Tamura, J.) Yes. A corporate decision to expose the public to serious danger when inexpensive alternatives exist is a legitimate basis for punitive damages. Punitive damages may be awarded not only for intentional torts, but also for conduct showing a conscious disregard of the rights of others. If a defendant was aware of the probable dangerous consequences of his acts but nonetheless proceeds ahead with his egregious conduct, punitives are permissible. Here, it was known to management that the placement of the fuel tank constituted a hazard, and that remedying the problem would have entailed inexpensive modifications. It is legitimate for a jury to find that such indifference to the rights of the public warrant punitive damages. Affirmed.

EDITOR'S ANALYSIS: Punitive damages have various rationales. One cited by the court was that they may serve as an unofficial regulatory mechanism. The court was of the opinion that fines imposed by the government were inadequate to deter questionable conduct, so punitive damages could fill this role.

NOTES:

TXO PRODUCTION CORP. v. ALLIANCE RESOURCES CORP.

61 U.S.L.W. 4766 (1993).

NATURE OF CASE: Appeal from award of punitive damages.

FACT SUMMARY: TXO (P) contended that the punitive damages it was ordered to pay violated the Due Precess Clause of the Fourteenth Amendment by being excessive and the product of an unfair procedure.

CONCISE RULE OF LAW: In determining whether a particular award is so grossly excessive as to violate the Due Process Clause, a general rule of reasonableness must be followed.

FACTS: TXO (P) filed a complaint against Alliance (D) for a declaratory judgment removing a cloud on title to an interest in oil and gas development rights. Alliance (D) filed a counterclaim for slander of title. According to the West Virginia Court of Appeals, TXO (P) knowingly and intentionally brought a frivolous declaratory judgment action when its real intent was to reduce royalty payments. The counterclaim for slander of title was subsequently tried to a jury. Alliance (D) introduced evidence that TXO (P) was a large company in its own right, that the amount of royalties TXO (P) sought to renegotiate were substantial, and that TXO (P) had engaged in similar nefarious activities in its business dealings in other parts of the country. The jury awarded $19,000 in actual damages and $10 million in punitive damages to Alliance (D). The court of appeals affirmed the awards. TXO (P) appealed, and the U.S. Supreme Court granted certiorari.

ISSUE: In determining whether a particular award is so grossly excessive as to violate the Due Process Clause, does a general concern of reasonableness properly enter into the constitutional calculus?

HOLDING AND DECISION: (Stevens, J.) Yes. In determining whether a particular award is so grossly excessive as to violate the Due Process Clause, a general concern of reasonableness properly enters into the constitutional calculus. A mathematical bright line between the constitutionally acceptable and unacceptable cannot be drawn. The dramatic disparity between the actual damages and the punitive award is not controlling in this case. The jury may have reasonably determined that TXO (P) set out on a malicious and fraudulent course to win back, either in whole or in part, the lucrative stream of royalties that it had ceded to Alliance (D). The punitive damages award is certainly large, but in light of the amount of money potentially at stake, the bad faith demonstrated by TXO (P), and TXO's (P) wealth, the award was not so grossly excessive as to be beyond the power of the state to allow. [TXO's (P) arguments that the award was a result of an unfair procedure were held meritless.] Affirmed.

CONCURRENCE: (Kennedy, J.) It is probable that the jury's verdict was motivated by a legitimate concern for punishing and deterring TXO (P), rather than by bias, passion, or prejudice. There was ample evidence of willful and malicious conduct by TXO (P) in this case, including prior lawsuits brought against TXO (P) by others who have accused it of simila misdeeds.

DISSENT: (O'Connor) The jury system long has been a guarantor of fairness, a bulwark against tyranny, and a source of civic values. Nonetheless, the risk of prejudice and bias remains a real one in every case. This is especially true in the area of punitive damages, where juries sometimes receive only vague and amorphous guidance. Due process at least requires judges to engage in searching review where the verdict discloses such great disproportions as to suggest the possibility of bias, caprice, or passion.

EDITOR'S ANALYSIS: As for the standard of review, the Court refused to apply a heightened standard of review, as TXO (P) requested, or a rational basis standard, as Alliance (D) requested. Assuming that fair procedures were followed in a punitive damages award, the Court stated that a judgment that is a product of the judicial process is entitled to a strong presumption of validity. The Court further stressed that there are persuasive reasons for suggesting that the presumption should be irrebuttable.

NOTES:

TRANSCONTINENTAL GAS PIPE LINE CORP. v.
AMERICAN NAT'L PETROLEUM CO.
763 S.W.2d 809 (Tex. App. 1988).

NATURE OF CASE: Appeal of an award of damages for breach of contract and good faith.

FACT SUMMARY: American National (ANPC) (P) received punitive damages from TRANSCO (D) based upon its breach of contract and interference with other ANPC (P) agreements.

CONCISE RULE OF LAW: Plaintiffs may only receive punitive damages for breach of an implied covenant if there is at least one finding of an independent tort with accompanying actual damages.

FACTS: ANPC (P) co-owned gas wells in the Gulf of Mexico. ANPC (P) contracted with TRANSCO (D) to sell the gas from those wells. TRANSCO (D) was obligated to buy a specified percentage of ANPC's (P) monthly and annual production. ANPC (P) also had other gas sales agreements with third parties. The agreement was subsequently modified in 1983 to allow TRANSCO (D) to reduce the price paid for the gas if it would be uneconomic to pay the contract price. This market-out provision decision was to be made solely by TRANSCO (D) but was required to be made honestly and in good faith. In 1985, after gas prices dropped drastically, TRANSCO (D) took steps to reduce its obligations to buy gas from ANPC (P) and from other parties. These steps included an agreement that TRANSCO (D) attempted to force gas producers to sign, which would waive liability claims against TRANSCO (D) and set a lower price. When ANPC (P) refused to sign the agreement, TRANSCO (D) refused to honor its contract. ANPC (P) sued for breach of contract, breach of the duty of good faith, and tortious interference with ANPC's (P) agreements with other parties. A jury awarded $3.8 million for breach of contract and $16 million in punitive damages for tortious interference. TRANSCO (D) appealed.

ISSUE: May plaintiffs be awarded punitive damages for breach of an implied covenant where there is no finding as to an amount of actual tort damages?

HOLDING AND DECISION: (Per curiam) No. Plaintiffs may only receive punitive damages for breach of an implied covenant if there is at least one finding of an independent tort with accompanying actual damages. Punitive damages are not recoverable for breach of contract. Gross negligence, malicious conduct, or intentional breach do not entitle the injured party to exemplary damages. The failure to act in good faith in the execution of a contract does not constitute a tort except in the case of insurance contracts, where there is a special relationship between the parties. Thus, ANPC's (P) breach of contract and good faith claims cannot form the basis for punitive damages. On the other hand, punitive damages may be awarded for tort actions, provided that the jury makes a finding as to the amount of actual tort damages to support the award. It is the duty of the plaintiff to allege, prove, and secure jury findings on the specific amount of damages sufficient to support an award of punitive damages. In this case, ANPC (P) failed to secure such a finding from the jury. Therefore, since there was no jury award for tortious interference, there was no basis on which to support the punitive damages award. Reversed as to the punitive damages award.

EDITOR'S ANALYSIS: This decision also overruled some of the contractual damages awarded to ANPC (P), finding that a limitation on remedies clause in the contract was effective despite TRANSCO's (D) bad faith. The decision's limited holding regarding the tort of bad-faith breach of contract is in accord with the majority position, although some states have allowed the tort for employment contracts as well as for insurance contracts. Personal injury lawyers have argued that the tort should encompass any bad-faith breach of contract where the plaintiff is subordinate to the defendant.

NOTES:

8

CHAPTER 8
ANCILLARY REMEDIES

QUICK REFERENCE RULES OF LAW

1. **Enforcing Coercive Orders: The Contempt Power.** Coercive contempt fines imposed during a civil proceeding between private parties are mooted when the underlying litigation is settled. (International Union, United Mine Workers v. Clinchfield Coal Co.)

2. **Enforcing Coercive Orders: The Contempt Power.** Incarceration pursuant to coercive contempt is not legitimate when it no longer has coercive power. (Catena v. Seidl)

3. **Enforcing Coercive Orders: The Contempt Power.** When a certain matter is under judicial scrutiny, removal of that matter for court jurisdiction constitutes contempt. (Griffin v. County School Board)

4. **The Collateral Bar Rule.** Disobedience of a court order is punishable by contempt even if the order is unconstitutional, unless the order has been vacated or reversed. (Walker v. City of Birmingham)

5. **The Rights of Third Parties.** A court has the inherent power to render a binding judgment between the parties to litigation through an injunctive order against a nonparty and may enforce that order with its contempt powers. (United States v. Hall)

6. **Collecting Money Judgments — Execution, Garnishment, and the Like.** Notice by a debtor to a sheriff when the sheriff is proceeding to attach or levy upon property is not notice to the creditor for whom the levy is made. (Credit Bureau of Broken Bow v. Moninger)

7. **Collecting Money Judgments — Execution, Garnishment, and the Like.** Garnishees are liable to garnisher creditors for all debts that the garnishee owes to the debtor at the time a writ of garnishment is filed. (Dixie National Bank v. Chase)

8. **Collecting Money Judgments — Coercive Collection of Money.** Social Security, disability, and pension benefits are not exempt from contempt and judgment proceedings for failure to pay child support or alimony. (In re Marriage of Logston)

9. **Preserving Assets before Judgment.** Plaintiffs seeking attachment must show that the defendant is about to dispose of property with the intent to frustrate enforcement of a judgment and that the claim has a probability of success on the merits. (City of New York v. CitiSource, Inc.)

10. **Preserving Assets before Judgment.** A receiver may only be appointed where income from a special fund is in actual danger of loss from neglect, waste, misconduct, or insolvency. (W.E. Erikson Construction v. Congress-Kenilworth Corp.)

11. **Litigation Expenses.** Attorney fees awards in civil rights actions are not required to be proportionate to the amount of damages. (City of Riverside v. Rivera)

12. **Litigation Expenses.** Courts may not enhance attorney fees above the lodestar amount in order to reflect the fact that the case was taken on a contingency fee basis. (City of Burlington v. Dague)

13. **Litigation Expenses.** Attorney fees in common fund cases may be determined by use of a percentage-of-the-fund method rather than a lodestar calculation. (Swedish Hospital Corp. v. Shalala)

14. **Litigation Expenses.** Courts are not required to reject settlements that include a waiver of attorney fees in civil rights litigation. (Evans v. Jeff D.)

INTERNATIONAL UNION, UNITED MINE WORKERS v. CLINCHFIELD COAL CO.

402 S.E.2d 899 (Va. App. 1991).

NATURE OF CASE: Appeal from an order denying a motion to vacate civil contempt fines.

FACT SUMMARY: The United Mine Workers Union (D) sought to have the civil contempt fines imposed by a court during a violent strike vacated when the strike was settled.

CONCISE RULE OF LAW: Coercive contempt fines imposed during a civil proceeding between private parties are mooted when the underlying litigation is settled.

FACTS: In 1989, the United Mine Workers Union (D) commenced a strike against Clinchfield (P) and other coal companies (P). The companies (P) filed a complaint that the Union (D) was violating Virginia's right-to-work law, and the court issued an injunction against certain strike-related activities. After numerous acts in violation of the injunction, including violence, took place, the court found the Union (D) in contempt and imposed fines totaling $64.13 million. The fines were directed to be paid to the coal companies (P), to the local counties involved, and to the commonwealth of Virginia. The Union (D) and the coal companies (P) settled the strike and moved to vacate the fines. The court vacated only the fines payable to the companies (P) and refused to vacate the others, which totaled $52 million. The Union (D) appealed.

ISSUE: Are coercive contempt fines imposed during a civil proceeding between private parties mooted when the underlying litigation is settled?

HOLDING AND DECISION: (Koontz, J.) Yes. Coercive contempt fines imposed during a civil proceeding between private parties are mooted when the underlying litigation is settled. Civil contempt sanctions may be divided into two categories: compensatory and coercive. Compensatory civil contempt sanctions attempt to compensate the plaintiff for losses sustained by noncompliance of a court order. Coercive contempt fines are imposed to force the defendant to comply. The court in the present case imposed mostly coercive civil contempt sanctions on the Union (D) since the coal companies (P) did not present any evidence of losses resulting from the Union's (D) noncompliance with the injunction. Although criminal contempt sanctions are unaffected by the resolution of the underlying dispute, both compensatory and coercive civil contempt fines are mooted when there is a settlement of the underlying litigation. A coercive contempt fine in a civil proceeding should not be treated as a criminal sanction, regardless of the nature of the act, because the underlying proceeding is civil. This rule still allows a court to maintain its authority. Accordingly, since the Union (D) and the coal companies (P) have settled the strike, the court must vacate all fines imposed in the civil proceedings. Reversed.

EDITOR'S ANALYSIS: The decision noted that the court could vindicate its authority through a subsequent criminal proceeding, which would afford the party alleged to be in contempt the appropriate constitutional safeguards. The Supreme Court of Virginia subsequently reversed this decision in Bagwell v. International Union, United Mine Workers, 423 S.E.2d 349 (Va. 1992), concluding that the courts must have the authority to enforce orders by employing coercive civil sanctions, or companies would merely delay paying fines until settlement rendered them moot. However, the appellate court's discussion regarding the difference between criminal, coercive, and compensatory civil contempt is in accord with most other jurisdictions.

NOTES:

CATENA v. SEIDL
N.J. Sup. Ct., 68 N.J. 224, 343 A.2d 744 (1975).

NATURE OF CASE: Appeal of trial court order expunging a civil contempt citation.

FACT SUMMARY: Catena (P), incarcerated for refusing to answer questions about mob activities, moved to have the contempt order nullified on the basis it had lost its coercive power.

CONCISE RULE OF LAW: Incarceration pursuant to coercive contempt is not legitimate when it no longer has coercive power.

FACTS: Catena (P), subpoenaed by a State (D) investigative agency, refused to answer questions regarding mob activities. He was cited for contempt and incarcerated. For several years he refused to talk. After several years Catena (P), in his 70s and in failing health, moved to expunge the contempt order, contending it had lost its coercive effect. The trial court ordered Catena (P) released, but the state supreme court vacated the order and remanded the action. The trial court found that the order had lost its coercive effect and ordered Catena (P) released. The State (D) appealed.

ISSUE: Is incarceration pursuant to coercive contempt legitimate when it no longer has coercive power?

HOLDING AND DECISION: (Per Curiam) No. Incarceration pursuant to coercive contempt is not legitimate when it no longer has coercive power. The whole purpose of coercive contempt is to compel an individual to do something. When it appears that the incarceration or other coercion is not going to do that for which it was instituted, it becomes a penalty, which is in the domain of criminal law. Here, it was clear, after five years, that Catena (P) was not going to talk, so the desired coercive effect of the contempt citation had failed. Affirmed.

DISSENT: (Schreiber, J.) Incarceration is inherently punitive, even in civil contempt, and the contempt order should not be vacated on the grounds the incarceration has taken on punitive characteristics. Traditionally, courts allowed incarceration pursuant to civil contempt to last indefinitely. The current trend, however, is to not allow open-ended contempt citations. In federal courts, for instance, the maximum term is 18 months. 18 U.S.C. § 1826.

EDITOR'S ANALYSIS: Generally speaking, contempt comes in two varieties, civil and criminal. The prior is coercive, the latter punitive. As a practical matter, civil contempt is often imposed for punitive reasons. The analytical distinction made by the court here is often lost on a trial court that believes itself to have been trifled with.

GRIFFIN v. COUNTY SCHOOL BOARD
363 F.2d 206 (4th Cir. 1966).

NATURE OF CASE: Contempt hearing based on disbursement of funds subject to judicial control.

FACT SUMMARY: The School Board of Prince Edward Co. (D) disbursed certain funds before the court of appeals could issue an order preventing it from doing so.

CONCISE RULE OF LAW: When a certain matter is under judicial scrutiny, removal of that matter for court jurisdiction constitutes contempt.

FACTS: The School Board of Prince Edward Co. (D) had been making certain tuition grants to segregated private schools. This was ordered stopped by a court. However, an issue remained as to whether certain disbursements for the previous year could still be made. The trial court did not prohibit the disbursements; an immediate appeal followed. Before the court of appeals could issue a decision, the disbursements were made. The Board (D) had reason to believe the appellate court would prohibit disbursements.

ISSUE: When a certain matter is under judicial scrutiny, does removal of that matter from court jurisdiction constitute contempt?

HOLDING AND DECISION: (Bryan, J.) Yes. When a certain matter is under judicial scrutiny removal of that matter from court jurisdiction constitutes contempt. Contempt is any action which tends to defeat a decree a court might make; it does not have to be an action contrary to a presently existing order. To take a matter away from court scrutiny is to challenge court authority. Here, the Board (D) divested itself of certain funds so that they would be beyond court reach, and this was with the intent of defeating court authority. The members of the Board (D) are in contempt.

DISSENT: (Haynsworth, C.J.) 18 U.S.C. § 401 limits contempt to disobedience of lawful writs or orders of a federal court. The statute does not mention the sort of situation found here. Since the statute limited rather than created the contempt power, a court should not go farther in finding contempt.

EDITOR'S ANALYSIS: The instant ruling was appealed, but the Supreme Court denied certiorari. A split in the circuits exists regarding the rule announced in Griffin. The Fifth Circuit, for instance, has held that an actual order must be disobeyed for contempt to exist. In re Stewart, 571 F.2d 958 (5th Cir. 1978).

WALKER v. CITY OF BIRMINGHAM
388 U.S. 307 (1967).

NATURE OF CASE: Appeal of contempt order issued pursuant to disobedience of a T.R.O.

FACT SUMMARY: Walker (D) and others disobeyed an anti-assembly T.R.O. obtained by the City of Birmingham (P), which then obtained a contempt citation.

CONCISE RULE OF LAW: Disobedience of a court order is punishable by contempt even if the order is unconstitutional, unless the order has been vacated or reversed.

FACTS: The City of Birmingham (P) obtained an ex parte T.R.O. prohibiting marches or assemblies. Walker (D) and others disobeyed the order. The City (P) then obtained a contempt citation against the marchers. Walker (D) appealed, contending that the order was unconstitutional and that, therefore, they were not bound to follow it. The Alabama Supreme Court rejected this and upheld the contempt citation. Walker (D) appealed to the U.S. Supreme Court.

ISSUE: Is disobedience of a court order punishable by contempt even if the order is unconstitutional, unless the order has been vacated or reversed?

HOLDING AND DECISION: (Stewart, J.) Yes. Disobedience of a court order is punishable by contempt even if the order is unconstitutional, unless the order has been vacated or reversed. Respect for rule of law demands that any order issued by a court of competent jurisdiction, however invalid, be obeyed. If an order is unconstitutional, the proper avenue of redress is to attack the order on appeal. A collateral attack upon a contempt citation is not the proper way to attack an invalid order. Here, the court issuing the order was of competent jurisdiction, and the order should have been obeyed until and unless it was reversed. Affirmed.

DISSENT: (Warren, C.J.) Constitutional protections cannot be evaded by turning an unconstitutional ordinance into an ex parte order. An unconstitutional order should not be given greater weight than an unconstitutional statute, which can be disobeyed and attacked.

DISSENT: (Douglas, J.) An order given by a court without jurisdiction need not be obeyed, and a court does not have jurisdiction to issue unconstitutional orders.

DISSENT: (Brennan, J.) The Court's opinion elevates arbitrary local judicial actions above constitutionally guaranteed rights, and this should not be so.

EDITOR'S ANALYSIS: As stated in the Court's opinion, a judicial order must be obeyed until reversed. The main exception to this is when the court lacks jurisdiction to issue the order. This is only true when the lack of jurisdiction is obvious; doubts are to be resolved in favor of jurisdiction. Justice Douglas' view of jurisdiction as stated in his dissent has not been adopted.

NOTES:

UNITED STATES v. HALL
472 F.2d 261 (5th Cir. 1973).

NATURE OF CASE: Appeal from judgment of criminal contempt.

FACT SUMMARY: Hall (D) was found to be in contempt of court for violating a restraining order in a school desegregation case.

CONCISE RULE OF LAW: A court has the inherent power to render a binding judgment between the parties to litigation through an injunctive order against a nonparty and may enforce that order with its contempt powers.

FACTS: In 1971, the district court issued an order directing the Duval County School Board to engage in a desegregation plan. In 1972, after complaints of attempted disruption to the implementation of that plan, the court entered a further, ex parte order enjoining all persons from so acting. The order provided that anyone with notice of the order who violates its terms would be subject to sanctions for contempt. Service of the order was effected on seven named, nonparties, including Hall (D). Hall (D) immediately took actions to violate the order and was arrested. He was found guilty of contempt in a nonjury trial, and sentenced to 60-days' imprisonment. He appealed on two grounds. First he contended that a nonparty who violates an injunction solely in pursuit of his own interests cannot be held in contempt. Second, he argued that Rule 65(d) of the Federal Rules of Civil Procedure limits the binding effect of injunctive orders to parties, their agents, and servants.

ISSUE: May a court validly issue and enforce an injunctive order against nonparties to the litigation in question?

HOLDING AND DECISION: (Wisdom, J.) Yes. Hall (D) pointed to several Supreme Court cases for his contention that a nonparty, acting alone, may not be held in contempt for violating a court order. However, those cases may be distinguished from the instant case in one important way. In the present case, the order enjoining nonparties from engaging in certain actions was necessary to effectuate a binding adjudication between the parties which were properly before the court. Thus, the court's initial order held that the black students had a right to a desegregated education and that the school board had the duty to provide it to them. The court retained the inherent power to restrain all persons from acting in such a manner as to impede the ability of the parties to carry out its desegregation order. This factor is what distinguished this case from those cited by Hall (D) in which the rights and duties of the parties, as between each other, were not affected by outside actions. It must be noted, however, that courts may not issue permanent injunctions against the entire world in cases of this kind. But where the order is necessarily temporary, as this one is, and where the enjoined party clearly had notice of the order, the court's action is proper. Likewise, Hall's (D) argument that F.R.C.P. 65(d) prevents the court's action, must fail. The Federal Rules were enacted as a codification of the common law powers of the federal courts. Although a suit such as the present one could not have been envisioned at common law, courts have always had the inherent power to protect its ability to render a binding judgment between the parties before it. The Federal Rules cannot be read as restricting that right. Affirmed.

EDITOR'S ANALYSIS: The court in Hall rested its decision partly on an analogy to the theory of in rem injunctions. In rem injunctions are generally made binding on all persons, regardless of notice, who come into contact with the property which is subject to the court's jurisdiction. Violation of the injunction may be punishable by contempt sanctions. However, the use of in rem injunctions has been widely criticized. As Professor Dobbs has noted, the punishment of someone who has violated an order without first receiving notice of the order may run into serious due process problems. See Dobbs, Contempt of Court: A Survey, 56 Conn. L. Rev. 183 (1971). Likewise, the Hall decision has also been subjected to criticism. Rendleman, Beyond Contempt: Obligors to Injunctions, 53 Tex. L. Rev. 873, 921-22 (1975).

NOTES:

CREDIT BUREAU OF BROKEN BOW v. MONINGER
204 Neb. 679, 284 N.W.2d 855 (1979).

NATURE OF CASE: Appeal from judgment affirming order awarding proceeds of sheriff's sale.

FACT SUMMARY: Credit Bureau of Broken Bow (P) appealed from a judgment affirming an order awarding proceeds of a sheriff's sale to the Bank (P), contending that as a lien creditor without knowledge of the Bank's (P) security interest it was entitled to the proceeds.

CONCISE RULE OF LAW: Notice by a debtor to a sheriff when the sheriff is proceeding to attach or levy upon property is not notice to the creditor for whom the levy is made.

FACTS: Credit Bureau of Broken Bow (the Bureau) (P) obtained a default judgment against Moninger (D). After this, Moninger (D) renewed his prior note with the Bank (P), which was to be secured by a security agreement, in part on Moninger's (D) pickup truck. The security agreement was not entered into at the time the loan was renewed. On June 28, 1978, at the Bureau's (P) request, a writ of execution was entered on the balance due on the default judgment. On July 7, 1978, the sheriff proceeded to execute on the pickup. Moninger (D) informed the sheriff that money had been borrowed from the Bank (D) against the pickup but the sheriff proceeded, executing on the pickup, even though he did not take possession of the vehicle or take the keys. On July 10, 1978, the Bank (P) and Moninger (D) executed a security agreement on the pickup. An action was brought for a determination of the division of the proceeds obtained from the sale of the pickup. From a decision in favor of the Bank (P), the Bureau (P) appealed, contending that it had a superior interest in the proceeds of the sheriff's sale.

ISSUE: Is notice by a debtor to a sheriff when he was proceeding to attach or levy upon property notice to the creditor for whom the levy is made?

HOLDING AND DECISION: (Brodkey, J.) No. Notice by a debtor to a sheriff when the sheriff is proceeding to attach or levy upon property is not notice to the creditor for whom the levy is made. (The court first determined that the sheriff had validly executed the levy by expressly asserting his dominion over the pickup, despite the fact that he did not take possession of the vehicle at the time of the levy.) The general rule is that an unperfected security interest is subordinate to the rights of a person who becomes a lien creditor without knowledge of the security interest. Peace officers are the agents of the law and are not ordinarily agents of the parties. To impute the knowledge of the sheriff to the Bureau (P) in this situation would result in unnecessary delays and place an undue burden on sheriffs. Since there was a valid levy, and the Bureau (P) had no

knowledge of the Bank's (P) interest in the pickup, and that interest was unperfected at the time of the levy, the Bureau (P) had prior rights to the proceeds of the sheriff's sale. Reversed and remanded.

EDITOR'S ANALYSIS: The U.C.C. provides the general rules of priority that apply in the present case, making the Bureau (P) the holder of the superior interest. The U.C.C. does not contain a provision which determines when a person obtains an execution lien. The states disagree over this point, and depending on the jurisdiction, a different result may be dictated.

NOTES:

DIXIE NATIONAL BANK v. CHASE
485 So. 2d 1353 (Fla. App. 1986).

NATURE OF CASE: Appeal from an award of damages under a writ of garnishment.

FACT SUMMARY: Chase (P) had the court issue a writ of garnishment to Dixie National Bank (D) against a debtor, Gore, but Dixie (D) failed to discover an account held by Gore.

CONCISE RULE OF LAW: Garnishees are liable to garnisher creditors for all debts that the garnishee owes to the debtor at the time a writ of garnishment is filed.

FACTS: In 1983, Chase (P) received a final judgment against Gore for $48,473 and shortly thereafter filed a writ of garnishment directed to Dixie National Bank (D). The court issued the writ and directed the garnishee, Dixie (D), to file an answer stating whether they were indebted to Gore at the time of writ. Dixie (D) responded that Gore had one account that contained only $32. However, Gore actually had another account at Dixie (D) that contained $13,870 at the time of the writ. Months later, Dixie (D) filed an amended answer that disclosed the other account, but in the meantime Gore had withdrawn nearly all of the money. Chase (P) brought suit against Dixie (D), and the trial court awarded Chase (P) $13,870 from Dixie (D), which appealed.

ISSUE: Are garnishees liable to garnisher creditors for all debts that the garnishee owes to the debtor at the time a writ of garnishment is filed?

HOLDING AND DECISION: (Hubbart, J.) Yes. Garnishees are liable to garnisher creditors for all debts that the garnishee owes to the debtor at the time a writ of garnishment is filed. Florida statute § 77.06(1) states that the service of a writ of garnishment makes the garnishee liable for all debts due by him to the defendant. Upon filing its answer, the garnishee is required to hold any moneys owed to the debtor. The garnishee is protected from any suit by the defendant debtor for garnishing funds where there is a good-faith doubt as to whether funds should be reported. This statute contemplates full disclosure by the garnishee so as to fully protect the creditor garnisher. If incomplete answers were permissible, there would be little incentive for full disclosure, and funds could be spirited away by a debtor. This would be contrary to the purpose of the law. Therefore, the garnishee is liable to the garnisher creditor for all debts that the garnishee owed to the debtor at the time of the writ. Accordingly, garnishee Dixie (D) was liable to Chase (P), a garnisher creditor, because Dixie (D) owed Gore $13,870 at the time of the writ. Affirmed.

EDITOR'S ANALYSIS: Typically, garnishees are banks or employers. The garnishee is permitted to defend this type of suit based upon the fact that it did not owe the debtor but cannot litigate the underlying judgment which the garnishee won. In some states, a garnishee who fails to answer a writ may be liable for the entire amount of the judgment, regardless of its actual liability to the debtor.

NOTES:

IN RE MARRIAGE OF LOGSTON
469 N.E.2d 167 (Ill. 1984).

NATURE OF CASE: Appeal of a contempt order.

FACT SUMMARY: Eugene Logston (D) contended that his Social Security, pension, and disability income were exempt from a contempt order to pay alimony arrearages to his ex-wife.

CONCISE RULE OF LAW: Social Security, disability, and pension benefits are not exempt from contempt and judgment proceedings for failure to pay child support or alimony.

FACTS: Eugene Logston (D) was married to Kate Logston from 1966 to 1981. Eugene (D) was ordered to pay Kate $221.50 per month for maintenance as part of the property settlement. Eugene (D) was retired due to a disability and received Social Security, pension, and disability payments for his income. Eugene (D) failed to make any payments through May 1983. Part of these arrearages were paid through judgment and garnishment proceedings, but Eugene (D) still owed $4,707 in May 1983. Kate instituted an action for the arrearages, and a contempt order was issued against Eugene (D). Eugene (D) responded that his income was exempt from contempt proceedings under Illinois law and appealed.

ISSUE: Are Social Security, disability, and pension benefits exempt from contempt and judgment proceedings for failure to pay child support or alimony?

HOLDING AND DECISION: (Ryan, J.) No. Social Security, disability, and pension benefits are not exempt from contempt and judgment proceedings for failure to pay child support or alimony. Illinois law does exempt Social Security, pension, and disability payments from judgment and attachment to satisfy debts. This law was enacted based on the policy that a creditor should not wholly deprive a person from supporting his family. However, the exemption statute is ambiguous as to whether it was designed to cover contempt proceedings. Illinois law has long recognized contempt as an appropriate sanction for willful failure to pay alimony or child support. Additionally, new legislation allows courts to garnish the income of a nonpaying former spouse regardless of the source of the income and exemption provisions. Therefore, the exemption statute is not a defense to a contempt order to pay alimony arrearages. The fact that a court enters a "judgment" for the amount should not alter this result. Thus, Eugene Logston (D) does not have a valid exemption from the contempt order. Affirmed.

EDITOR'S ANALYSIS: This decision also rejected Eugene's (D) argument that his failure to pay was not willful since he was unable to make the payments. The court noted that Eugene (D) had failed to prove that his income was spent on only bare living expenses. Under the contempt order in this case, Eugene (D) was to be imprisoned if he did not make the arrearages payment in thirty days. Most states would permit installment payments in circumstances like Eugene's (D).

NOTES:

CITY OF NEW YORK v. CITISOURCE, INC.
679 F. Supp. 393 (S.D.N.Y. 1988).

NATURE OF CASE: Appeal from judgment vacating an order for attachment.

FACT SUMMARY: New York City (P) sought to attach a bank account held by persons who were involved in a bribery scheme so that they could not dispose of the money before a civil RICO action was decided.

CONCISE RULE OF LAW: Plaintiffs seeking attachment must show that the defendant is about to dispose of property with the intent to frustrate enforcement of a judgment and that the claim has a probability of success on the merits.

FACTS: In 1986, Friedman (D) and Kaplan (D) were found guilty of criminal charges of racketeering, RICO conspiracy, and mail fraud in a bribery scheme to influence the award of a city contract to Citisource (D). New York City (P) filed a civil RICO action against Friedman (D), Kaplan (D), and Citisource (D). Kaplan (D) and Friedman (D) then called the European American Bank, where they held large accounts and inquired about withdrawing the money. New York City (P) then moved for an attachment of the assets of Friedman (D) and Kaplan (D). The trial court granted the attachment, but the court of appeals reversed. New York City (P) appealed.

ISSUE: Must plaintiffs seeking attachment show that the defendant is about to dispose of property with the intent to frustrate enforcement of a judgment and that the claim has a probability of success on the merits?

HOLDING AND DECISION: (Conner, J.) Yes. Plaintiffs seeking attachment must show that the defendant is about to dispose of property with the intent to frustrate enforcement of a judgment and that the claim has a probability of success on the merits. New York Civil Practice Law and Rules § 6201(3) provides for an attachment when the defendant in a civil action, with intent to frustrate the enforcement of a judgment that might be rendered in the plaintiff's favor, disposes of, or attempts to remove, assets. This is a harsh remedy, so the supporting evidence must be strictly construed against the party seeking the attachment. Fraud will not be lightly inferred. The plaintiff must show that the defendants have attempted to conceal their property. The timing of an action by the defendant may give rise to an inference that there was an intent to frustrate judgment enforcement. Friedman (D) and Kaplan's (D) actions regarding their assets occurred immediately following their realization of potential civil liability. Thus, an inference of an intent to frustrate enforcement has been raised by New York City (P). Kaplan (D) and Friedman (D) failed to produce evidence to refute this inference. The other requirement for an attachment under § 6201(3) is that the underlying claim has a probability of success on the merits. When

a contract is procured through bribes, the defrauded party is entitled to recover as damages the value of the bribes. Therefore, given the collateral estoppel effect of the criminal convictions of Kaplan (D) and Friedman (D), New York City (P) is likely to win on the merits of its civil RICO action. Thus, the attachment was appropriate in this case. Motion granted.

EDITOR'S ANALYSIS: In most states, attachments refers to a levy or garnishment of assets before a judgment is reached. The general rule in most jurisdictions is that attachment is allowed where there is a threat that the assets will disappear. Federal Rule of Civil Procedure 64 authorizes federal district courts to apply state attachment rules.

NOTES:

W.E. ERICKSON CONSTRUCTION v. CONGRESS-KENILWORTH CORP.

445 N.E.2d 1209 (Ill. App. 1983).

NATURE OF CASE: Interlocutory appeal from an order appointing a receiver in breach of contract action.

FACT SUMMARY: Erickson (P) constructed a water slide amusement for Congress-Kenilworth (D) and then sought to appoint a receiver when Congress-Kenilworth (D) was unable to pay for the construction.

CONCISE RULE OF LAW: A receiver may only be appointed where income from a special fund is in actual danger of loss from neglect, waste, misconduct, or insolvency.

FACTS: In 1981, Congress-Kenilworth (D) hired Erickson (P), a general contractor, to construct a water slide amusement for a total cost of $535,000. When the project was 60% complete, Erickson (P) applied for a partial payment of $246,958, which Congress-Kenilworth (D) was unable to pay. The parties agreed that, in lieu of payment, Congress-Kenilworth (D) would deliver, to Erickson (P), the deed to the property where the water slide was located as a form of security. The project was completed and opened to the public in the summer of 1981. Congress-Kenilworth (D) paid a total of $150,000 to Erickson (P) in 1981. In August 1981, it was discovered that the Department of the Army actually owned the real property and that the water slide was an encroachment. A receiver was appointed by the court after a finding that the security deed given to Erickson (P) was worthless and that the water slide was bringing in hundreds of thousands of dollars while Congress-Kenilworth (D) was contending that it had no assets. Congress-Kenilworth (D) appealed the order appointing a receiver.

ISSUE: May a receiver be appointed where there is a speculative fear that income from a special fund will be diverted?

HOLDING AND DECISION: (Jiganti, J.) No. A receiver may only be appointed where income from a special fund is in actual danger of loss from neglect, waste, misconduct, or insolvency. Appointment of a receiver is a high and extraordinary remedy which deprives the legal owner of possession. It must be exercised with caution, and only when a court is satisfied there is an imminent danger of loss if it is not exercised. The general rule is that an applicant must have a clear right to the property or have some lien upon it. Secondly, the property must have been obtained by the defendant by fraud, or the income arising from the property must be in danger of loss from neglect, waste, misconduct, or insolvency. Erickson (P) was able to meet the first requirement because the property deed was given as security for the payments owed to Erickson (P), giving rise to an equitable lien because there was a mutual mistake as to the validity of the deed. However, Erickson (P) only alleged a fear of diversion of the

income from the water slide. A speculative fear is not legally sufficient to support the drastic remedy of the appointment of a receiver. Thus, the second prong of the receivership requirements was not met by Erickson (P), and the appointment was improperly granted. Reversed and remanded.

EDITOR'S ANALYSIS: On remand, a trial was held on many different issues, including construction defects and the costs of the receivership. Eventually, the court ruled that Erickson (P) was entitled to payment minus $67,000 in damages caused by the receivership. Appointment of a receiver is similar to an attachment proceeding but allows an experienced businessperson to continue an operation.

NOTES:

CITY OF RIVERSIDE v. RIVERA
477 U.S. 561 (1986).

NATURE OF CASE: Appeal of an award of attorney fees in civil rights action for damages.

FACT SUMMARY: The district court awarded attorney fees that far exceeded the judgment for damages in a civil rights suit.

CONCISE RULE OF LAW: Attorney fees awards in civil rights actions are not required to be proportionate to the amount of damages.

FACTS: Rivera (P) and eight other Chicano individuals sued the City of Riverside (D) and individual police officers (D) who broke into their home without a search warrant and used unnecessary physical force. A jury awarded Rivera (P) and the others (P) a total of $66,000 for their constitutional claims. Rivera (P) also sought attorney fees under Section 1988 of the Civil Rights Attorney's Fees Awards Act, which authorizes attorney fees to prevailing parties in civil rights actions. The trial court awarded Rivera's (P) attorneys $245,456 based upon 1,946 hours of work. Riverside (D) appealed the award of attorney fees.

ISSUE: Must attorney fees awards in civil rights actions be proportionate to the amount of damages?

HOLDING AND DECISION: (Brennan, J.) No. Attorney fees awards in civil rights actions are not required to be proportionate to the amount of damages. According to the American Rule, each party to a lawsuit ordinarily bears its own attorney fees. However, under § 1988, Congress has authorized district courts to award reasonable attorney fees to prevailing parties in civil rights action. A reasonable fee is determined by multiplying the number of hours reasonably spent by a reasonable hourly rate, a figure commonly known as the "lodestar." Congress did not intend for the amount of attorney fees to be proportionate to the amount of damages that a plaintiff recovers. Section 1988 was intended to serve the public interest because successful civil rights plaintiffs often secure important social benefits that are not reflected in the amount of damages. The amount awarded to Rivera's (P) attorneys was reasonable because the district court properly used the lodestar formula. Accordingly, the attorney fees award was proper even though it was disproportionate to the amount of damages in this case. Affirmed.

CONCURRENCE: (Powell, J.) A court may consider the vindication of constitutional rights and, by extension, the public interest in addition to the amount of damages recovered.

DISSENT: (Burger, J.) $125 an hour is far too much to pay for the services of two attorneys like Rivera's (P) who had recently graduated from law school and only had three years of experience between them.

DISSENT: (Rehnquist, J.) The lodestar formula contemplates that only hours reasonably expended by the attorneys should be compensated. It was not reasonable for Rivera's (P) attorneys to spend 1,900 hours to recover a very small amount.

EDITOR'S ANALYSIS: This case demonstrates one of the federal statutory exemptions to the otherwise firmly entrenched American rule that each party is responsible for its own attorney fees. The viability of the American rule is based on the policy that litigation should not be discouraged. Moreover, as this case demonstrates, the cost and time taken up by trials to determine a fair fee would be administratively burdensome.

NOTES:

CITY OF BURLINGTON v. DAGUE
112 S. Ct. 2638 (1992).

NATURE OF CASE: Appeal of an award of attorney fees.

FACT SUMMARY: After successfully prosecuting a case against Burlington (D), Dague (P) was awarded attorney fees for a suit against Burlington (D) which the trial judge enhanced by 25% to reflect the fact that attorneys took the case on a contingent fee basis and there was a substantial risk of not prevailing.

CONCISE RULE OF LAW: Courts may not enhance attorney fees above the lodestar amount in order to reflect the fact that the case was taken on a contingency fee basis.

FACTS: Dague (P) owned land adjacent to a landfill operated by Burlington (D). Dague (P) sued Burlington (D) under the Solid Waste Disposal Act and the Federal Water Pollution Control Act, and the trial court ruled that Burlington (D) must close the landfill. The court determined that Dague (P) was the substantially prevailing party and was entitled to an award of attorney fees. Dague (P) presented figures for the number of hours and the hourly rate for the attorneys, and the court accepted a lodestar amount of $198,027. The court then declared that this amount would be enhanced by 25%, or $49,506, because the case had been taken on a contingency fee basis and the risk of Dague (P) not prevailing was substantial. Burlington (D) appealed this award.

ISSUE: May courts enhance attorney fees above the lodestar amount in order to reflect the fact that the case was taken on a contingency fee basis?

HOLDING AND DECISION: (Scalia, J.) No. Courts may not enhance attorney fees above the lodestar amount in order to reflect the fact that the case was taken on a contingency fee basis. Reasonable attorney fees are authorized by many federal statutes to be awarded to the prevailing party. In Delaware Valley I, 478 U.S. 546 (1986), the Court established that the lodestar amount is presumed to represent a reasonable fee. The lodestar figure is computed by multiplying a reasonable hourly rate by a reasonable number of hours spent on the case, taking into account the nature and difficulty of the litigation. A party that seeks to enhance or decrease the lodestar has the burden of proving that an adjustment is necessary to produce a reasonable fee. An enhancement for a contingency fee–type case would duplicate factors that already are considered in the lodestar amount. In a difficult case, either a higher number of hours will have to be spent, or a more experienced or skilled attorney who charges a higher rate will be necessary. The relative merits of a claim should not play a factor in the determination of reasonable fees because if fees were enhanced based upon the difficulty of winning a case, nonmeritorious claims might be encouraged.

Furthermore, the interest in ready administrability and concerns about avoiding burdensome satellite litigation make the lodestar approach without enhancement superior. Accordingly, the district court's decision to award Dague (P) an enhancement on its lodestar figure because of the relative merits of the claim was improper. Reversed.

DISSENT: (Blackmun, J.) The enhancement was proper and consistent with the intent of Congress, whose purpose in adopting the provision was to strengthen the enforcement of selected federal laws by ensuring that competent counsel would be available. Reasonable enhancements must be allowed so that attorneys will continue to take cases that may be difficult to win.

EDITOR'S ANALYSIS: Justice Blackmun's dissent also noted that determining the lodestar amount is actually no easier in practice to ascertain and that the enhancement in the present case only became time-consuming after the Court allowed review. The factors in setting the lodestar figure include the undesirability of the case, which would seem to take into account the relative merits of the claim. In any event, the merits of a claim do not dictate contingent fees in actual private practice; attorneys merely charge a standard percentage and turn down all cases they deem too risky at that amount.

NOTES:

SWEDISH HOSPITAL CORP. v. SHALALA
1 F.3d 1261 (D.C. Cir. 1993).

NATURE OF CASE: Appeal of an award of attorney fees.

FACT SUMMARY: The presiding court in a suit against the Department of Health and Human Services (HHS) (D) awarded the attorneys for a group of hospitals (P) a percentage of the damages rather than a lodestar amount.

CONCISE RULE OF LAW: Attorney fees in common fund cases may be determined by use of a percentage-of-the-fund method rather than a lodestar calculation.

FACTS: A class of hospitals (P) challenged a rule of the Department of Health and Human Services (D) that required the hospitals to pay for photocopying costs involved in mandatory peer review of treatments covered by Medicare. The case was settled in favor of the hospitals (P) for approximately $28 million. The attorneys for the hospitals (P) filed a fee petition for 20% of the settlement. HHS (D) responded that they should only be entitled to a lodestar amount of $619,000. The district court awarded the percentage of the fund to the attorneys, and HHS (D) appealed.

ISSUE: May attorney fees in common fund cases be determined by use of a percentage-of-the-fund method rather than a lodestar calculation?

HOLDING AND DECISION: (Sentelle, J.) Yes. Attorney fees in common fund cases may be determined by use of a percentage-of-the-fund method rather than a lodestar calculation. An early exception to the general rule that each party must pay their own legal costs was the common fund doctrine in class actions. Under this doctrine, attorneys for a class who created a common fund for the class may be reimbursed for the fund. Courts have considerable discretion in determining attorney fees. Since application of the percentage of the fund method resulted in large fee awards, a trend toward alternative calculations began in the 1970's. The lodestar amount, which is a reasonable hourly rate multiplied by a reasonable number of hours, emerged as the prevailing method of fee calculation. However, there are deficiencies in the lodestar process, including creating a disincentive for settlements, as well as confusion and inconsistency in its administration. These problems are present in common fund cases, where the lodestar approach gives attorneys incentive to spend as many hours as possible on a case. The percentage-of-the-fund method of calculation, whereby attorneys are awarded a specified percentage of the fund which is created, has fewer problems. It more accurately reflects the economics of litigation practice, is much easier to calculate, and is less subjective. Therefore, the percentage of the fund method may be used in common fund cases. The 20% of the settlement fund awarded to the attorneys for the class of hospitals (P) was within the reasonable range in similar cases. Therefore, the court was acting within its discretion to set reasonable fees. Affirmed.

DISSENT: (Ginsburg, J.) The Supreme Court's decision in City of Burlington v. Dague, 112 S.Ct. 2638 (1992), makes it clear that the lodestar approach is the appropriate starting point for fees and more clearly reflects a reasonable fee. Courts must have a special reason for deviating significantly from the lodestar figure.

EDITOR'S ANALYSIS: Lawyers who recover a fund in which other parties will take a portion may recover fees whether or not an actual class-action suit was filed. The common fund percentage rule is actually an extension of the general restitution rule for these type of situations. Some commentators have argued that attorneys who confer benefits on third parties are acting as volunteers and should have no right to a percentage.

NOTES:

EVANS v. JEFF D.
475 U.S. 717 (1986).

NATURE OF CASE: Appeal of court approval of the settlement of a civil rights action.

FACT SUMMARY: The public officials (D) responsible for the education of handicapped children (P) sought to settle a civil rights action by agreeing to virtually all of the injunctive relief conditioned on a waiver of attorney fees.

CONCISE RULE OF LAW: Courts are not required to reject settlements that include a waiver of attorney fees in civil rights litigation.

FACTS: A class of handicapped children (P) filed a complaint based on the deficiencies in the educational and health care services provided by state public officials (D). The district court appointed Johnson, a public interest attorney, to prosecute the action. One week before the civil rights trial was scheduled to begin, the public officials (D) offered a proposal to the children (P) which included virtually all of the injunctive relief which had been sought in the complaint. However, the offer included a waiver of any claim to attorney fees for Johnson or legal costs. Johnson determined that it was his ethical obligation to accept the settlement conditioned on the district court's approval. Johnson filed a motion requesting that the court approve the settlement except for the fee waiver. The court rejected the motion and approved the settlement with the children's (P) fee waiver intact. The court of appeals, however, invalidated the fee waiver and left the remainder of the settlement standing. The public officials (D) appealed.

ISSUE: Are courts required to reject settlements that include a waiver of attorney fees?

HOLDING AND DECISION: (Stevens, J.) No. Courts are not required to reject settlements that include a waiver of attorney fees in civil rights litigation. In other words, courts may refuse to award fees. Under Rule 23, courts have the power to approve or reject settlements negotiated by the parties, but courts are not authorized to require parties to accept settlements to which they have not agreed. The Civil Rights Fees Act does not require a court to disapprove a settlement that is conditioned on waiver of statutory eligibility for attorney fees. Therefore, the district court did not abuse its discretion in approving the fee waiver. The statutory eligibility for attorney fees for the prevailing party in civil rights litigation does not prevent a party from waiving the right. A general rule against waiver would impede vindication of civil rights because the attractiveness of settlements would be reduced. Since the potential liability for fees in this type of litigation is very great, fee awards must be allowed into the bargaining process. Parties seek to fix their liability through settlement, and many cases will not be settled if the liability for fees remains open.

Accordingly, the acceptance of the settlement and its complete fee waiver for the class of handicapped children (P) represented by Johnson was not an abuse of discretion by the district court. Reversed.

DISSENT: (Brennan, J.) Congress' purpose in allowing for attorney fees in civil rights actions was to provide for effective public enforcement through the availability of competent counsel. Negotiated fee waivers will diminish lawyers' expectations of receiving fees and will decrease the willingness of lawyers to accept civil rights cases. Since this result is the exact opposite of what Congress sought to achieve through the Fees Act, fee waivers must be prohibited.

EDITOR'S ANALYSIS: This decision has not had the impact that the bar expected. Many civil rights attorneys have begun to interpret their ethical obligations differently and refuse to negotiate fee waivers. Others draft contracts in which the client agrees not to accept a fee waiver. Still, it seems that there is an inherent conflict of interest between the attorney and the client where fees are negotiated at the same time as the underlying claim.

NOTES:

CHAPTER 9
REMEDIAL DEFENSES

QUICK REFERENCE RULES OF LAW

1. **Unclean Hands and in Pari Delicto.** Defendants may only use the in pari delicto defense when the plaintiff is an active and voluntary participant in the unlawful activity that is the subject of the suit. (Pinter v. Dahl)

2. **Unconscionability and the Equitable Contract Defenses.** Even though a contract may be perfectly legal, entitling both parties to legal relief, equity will not provide specific relief to any party who has driven too hard a bargain or obtained too one-sided an agreement. (Campbell Soup Co. v. Wentz)

3. **Estoppel and Waiver.** A party is equitably estopped from asserting rights which it has knowingly acted adversely to and has induced a change in position by the other party by such action. (United States v. Georgia-Pacific Co.)

4. **Estoppel and Waiver.** An admission by an insurance carrier of partial liability for a loss does not constitute a waiver of any other coverage defenses. (United States Fidelity & Guaranty Co. v. Bimco Iron & Metal Corp.)

5. **Laches.** Laches bars a suit where a substantial delay by the plaintiff prejudices the defendant. (National Association for the Advancement of Colored People v. N.A.A.C.Pc Legal Defense & Educational Fund)

6. **Statutes of Limitations.** A statute of limitations does not bar a suit where there is a continuing violation against the plaintiff. (Baker v. F & F Investment Co.)

7. **Statutes of Limitations.** The statute of limitations period for personal injuries begins to run at the time the plaintiff has knowledge of the injury, of the operative cause of the injury, and of the causative relationship between the injury and the operative conduct. (O'Brien v. Eli Lilly & Co.)

8. **Statutes of Limitations.** Equitable estoppel sufficient to bar the application of the statute of limitations results from fraudulent concealment of an action which is unknown to a party. (Knaysi v. A. H. Robins Co.)

PINTER v. DAHL
486 U.S. 622 (1988).

NATURE OF CASE: Appeal of a judgment allowing rescission of a securities transaction.

FACT SUMMARY: Pinter (D) sought to defend an action for rescission under federal securities laws on the basis that Dahl (P), the buyer, was equally at fault for the illegality.

CONCISE RULE OF LAW: Defendants may only use the in pari delicto defense when the plaintiff is an active and voluntary participant in the unlawful activity that is the subject of the suit.

FACTS: Pinter (D), an oil and gas producer, met with Dahl (P), a real estate broker, about investing in oil and gas leases. Dahl (P) invested $310,000 in Pinter's (D) Black Gold Oil Company to acquire properties. Dahl (P) then solicited other purchasers to invest money in the venture but received no commission in connection with these investments. Pinter (D) subsequently sold the participating interests without registering them under the Securities Act. When the venture failed, Dahl (P) filed suit against Pinter (D) seeking rescission for selling unregistered securities. The trial court denied Pinter's (D) in pari delicto defense that Dahl (P) should not recover because he was equally at fault. Pinter (D) appealed.

ISSUE: May defendants use the in pari delicto defense when the plaintiff is partially at fault for the underlying illegality?

HOLDING AND DECISION: (Blackmun, J.) No. Defendants may only use the in pari delicto defense when the plaintiff is an active and voluntary participant in the unlawful activity that is the subject of the suit. The equitable defense of in pari delicto, which literally means "in equal fault," is rooted in the common law notion that a plaintiff's recovery may be barred by his own wrongful conduct. Traditionally, the defense was limited to situations in which the plaintiff bore at least substantially equal responsibility for the injury and where his culpability arose out of the same illegal act. Now the in pari delicto defense is applied to situations encompassed under the "unclean hands" doctrine. This doctrine is premised on the ground that judicial relief should be denied to wrongdoers as an effective means of deterring illegality. In order to have substantially equal responsibility, the plaintiff must be an active, voluntary participant in the unlawful activity that is the subject of the suit, and the degree of fault must be essentially indistinguishable. In the context of an action under federal securities laws against selling unregistered securities, a purchaser's knowledge that the securities are unregistered cannot, by itself, constitute equal culpability. There must be some degree of cooperation between the seller and the buyer in carrying out the scheme. Additionally, the in pari delicto defense is not available when there would be interference with the underlying purpose of the securities laws. Precluding suits by plaintiffs who are primarily investors would interfere with enforcement of securities laws. Thus, the plaintiff's role in the offering or sale of unregistered securities must be more as a promoter than as an investor in order to invoke the in pari delicto defense. The record in this case does not indicate whether Dahl's (P) participation rose to the level necessary for Pinter (D) to assert the in pari delicto defense. Accordingly, the case is remanded.

DISSENT: (Stevens, J.) Although the majority is correct is setting the standard for using the defense, Pinter (D) never suggested during the trial that Dahl (P) played any role in the failure to register the securities. The majority has now given him a chance to relitigate an issue he should have addressed in district court.

EDITOR'S ANALYSIS: As the decision noted, the in pari delicto defense is very similar to the unclean hands maxim of equity. While the unclean hands defense may only be asserted in equitable actions, in pari delicto is available as a defense in legal suits, such as the one for damages in Dahl's (P) complaint. For a discussion of unclean hands, see Zechariah Chafee, Jr., Coming into Equity with Clean Hands, 47 Mich. L. Rev. 877 (1949).

NOTES:

CAMPBELL SOUP CO. v. WENTZ
172 F.2d 80 (3d Cir. 1948).

NATURE OF CASE: Appeal from dismissal of breach of contract action for specific relief.

FACT SUMMARY: Wentz (D) contracted to sell carrots to Campbell (P) but instead sold them to Lojeski (D).

CONCISE RULE OF LAW: Even though a contract may be perfectly legal, entitling both parties to legal relief, equity will not provide specific relief to any party who has driven too hard a bargain or obtained too one-sided an agreement.

FACTS: On June 21, 1947, Wentz (D) contracted to sell all the Chantenay red cored carrots to be grown on a certain fifteen-acre parcel of his farm to Campbell (P) for a price between $23 and $30 per ton. The contract, drawn up by and in the primary interest of Campbell (P), provided several conditions. Paragraph 2 set out a very particular manner of delivery and further stated that Campbell (P) was to be judge of conformance with all specifications. Paragraphs 3 and 4 provided that Campbell (P) could refuse all carrots in excess of twelve tons per acre but that Wentz (D) could only sell such excess carrots after Campbell (P) rejected them. Paragraph 9 provided certain circumstances under which Campbell (P) would be excused from accepting delivery of any carrots but provided that, even if it was, Wentz (D) could not sell the carrots elsewhere without Campbell's (P) approval. By January 1948, the price of Chantenay carrots had risen to $90 per ton. Wentz (D) thereupon notified Campbell (P) that it would no longer deliver carrots to them, selling instead to Lojeski (D), a neighbor, who in turn sold to Campbell (P). Campbell instituted this action, as a result, for specific performance of its contract with Wentz (D). The trial court dismissed, and this appeal followed.

ISSUE: May a court of equity deny specific relief to a party to a wholly legal contract merely because he has obtained a markedly one-sided agreement?

HOLDING AND DECISION: (Goodrich, J.) Yes. Even though a contract may be perfectly legal, entitling both parties to legal relief, equity will not provide specific relief to any party who has driven too hard a bargain or obtained too one-sided an agreement. The general policy of liberality in the granting of specific relief favors the granting of it as long as the court is not forced to undertake too burdensome or time-consuming a supervisory role in the process. As such, the trial court below erred in dismissing the suit because of the purported adequacy of the legal remedy here. (The relative "uniqueness" of these carrots is really immaterial.) But the dismissal was nevertheless proper considering the excessively burdensome provisional that Campbell (P) obtained in its contract with Wentz (D). Affirmed.

EDITOR'S ANALYSIS: This case points up what has been termed "equity's middle course" in the question of whether courts should enforce contracts which, though unfair, fall short of being unconscionable. Essentially equitable (though not legal) relief will be denied wherever the evidence supports a finding of misrepresentation, unclean hands (from overreaching), inadequate consideration, equitable estoppel, etc. Note also, here, the fact that the court skirts the question of adequacy of the legal remedy which the trial court had held dispositive below. As a general rule, inadequacy of the legal remedy (i.e., damages) must be established before a party may obtain equitable relief. "Uniqueness" of the subject matter of a contract (carrots, above) will often make damages inadequate. In Campbell, the court in essence said that the mere need for product uniformity by Campbell (P) in its soups made Wentz's (D) Chantenay red carrots unique.

NOTES:

UNITED STATES v. GEORGIA-PACIFIC CO.
421 F.2d 92 (9th Cir. 1970).

NATURE OF CASE: Appeal from denial of declaratory relief.

FACT SUMMARY: Georgia-Pacific (D) contended that the Government (P) was equitably estopped from asserting a right to land after manifesting an intent to reject the contract under which it claimed title.

CONCISE RULE OF LAW: A party is equitably estopped from asserting rights which it has knowingly acted adversely to and has induced a change in position by the other party by such action.

FACTS: Georgia-Pacific's (D) predecessor in title contracted with the Government (P) agreeing to allow land to be added to the Siskiyou National Forest. The land would remain privately owned until all timber was cleared at which time title would pass to the Government (P). The Government (P) was to provide fire protection from the date of the contract. Twenty years later, prior to the clearing of all timber, the Government (P) retracted the boundaries of the forest to exclude the land, and withdrew all fire protection. Four years later, Georgia-Pacific (D) purchased the land, and the Government (P) sued for specific performance of the original contract requiring conveyance of the land to it. The trial court held for Georgia-Pacific (D), finding a lack of consideration. The court of appeals affirmed, and the Government (P) appealed.

ISSUE: Is a party whose actions induce another to change his position in reliance on such actions equitably estopped from assuming an inconsistent position?

HOLDING AND DECISION: (Levin, J.) Yes. A party is estopped from adopting inconsistent positions after acting to induce another to act to his detriment. Here the Government (P) withdrew all fire protection from the land. Such was the consideration for the original contract. This withdrawal manifested an intent not to honor the contract and induced the owner to sell the land. Thus the Government (P) is equitably estopped from asserting its waived rights. Affirmed.

EDITOR'S ANALYSIS: Specific performance is of course an equitable remedy and as such is available only in the court's discretion. As with an equitable relief, a balancing of equities is performed to determine whether it is fair to grant the relief. Where the plaintiff has acted inequitably, it is unlikely equitable relief will be granted.

NOTES:

UNITED STATES FIDELITY & GUARANTY CO. v. BIMCO IRON & METAL CORP.
464 S.W.2d 353 (Tex. 1971).

NATURE OF CASE: Appeal from recovery of insurance benefits.

FACT SUMMARY: Bimco (P) contended United States Fidelity (USF) (D) waived its right to deny coverage based on Bimco's (P) failure to timely file a proof of loss because it admitted partial liability on the loss.

CONCISE RULE OF LAW: An admission by an insurance carrier of partial liability for a loss does not constitute a waiver of any other coverage defenses.

FACTS: Bimco (P) held an insurance policy from USF (D), covering it for property damage from vandals, but not for theft. Vandals broke into Bimco's (P) building, causing property damage and stealing property. USF (D) contended it was only responsible for the property damage and not for the theft. Bimco (P) sued, and USF (D) defended based on the policy language and on the failure of Bimco (P) to file a timely proof of loss. Bimco (P) contended USF (D) waived the late filing defense by admitting liability for the property damage. The trial court found all the damage to be property damage and entered judgment for Bimco (P). The court of appeals reversed, and Bimco (P) appealed.

ISSUE: Does an admission by an insurance carrier of partial liability for a loss constitute a waiver of all other coverage defenses?

HOLDING AND DECISION: (McGee, J.) No. An admission by an insurance carrier of liability for a part of a loss does not constitute a waiver of all other coverage defenses. The carrier denied liability for the theft based on the scope of the policy. Thus, failure to timely file a proof of loss was not dispositive of the issue. Further, there was no evidence introduced indicating any intent to waive all policy defenses. Therefore, the court of appeals decision must be affirmed.

EDITOR'S ANALYSIS: The court in this case makes two important points regarding the concept of waiver. First, an effective waiver of an affirmative right must be a clear and intentional act. Absent such actual or implied intent, no waiver has occurred. The second is the noted distinction between the concept of waiver and the concept of estoppel. As previously stated a waiver is the knowing relinquishment of a known right. Estoppel is the imposed preclusion of the exercise of a right.

NOTES:

NAACP v. NAACP LEGAL DEFENSE & EDUCATIONAL FUND

753 F.2d 131 (D.C. Cir. 1985).

NATURE OF CASE: Appeal of an injunction preventing use of a trademark.

FACT SUMMARY: The NAACP (P) sought to bar the Legal Defense Fund (D), a separate entity, from using the NAACP name although it had permitted use of its name for twelve years without objection.

CONCISE RULE OF LAW: Laches bars a suit where a substantial delay by the plaintiff prejudices the defendant.

FACTS: In 1939 the NAACP (P) created a separate organization, the NAACP Legal Defense Fund (LDF) (D), to perform the Association's (P) legal work in order to allow contributors to receive tax deductions. From 1940 to 1957, the LDF (D) was a subsidiary of the Association (P). In 1957, the groups mutually agreed to make the LDF (D) independent, although there were still coordinated efforts. Donations made to the wrong organization were forwarded to the intended beneficiary. However, as competition for fund-raising became more intense, the Association (P) passed a resolution that the LDF (D) should be forced to change its name to drop the NAACP in 1965. The Association (P) never brought a suit and remained silent about the LDF's (D) use of the name between 1966 and 1978. In 1982, the Association (P) registered the NAACP name as a trademark and initiated a suit against the LDF (D), which responded that the suit should be barred by laches. The district court granted an injunction to the Association (P), and the LDF (D) appealed.

ISSUE: Is a suit barred by the defense of laches where the plaintiff's delay has prejudiced the defendant?

HOLDING AND DECISION: (Bazelon, J.) Yes. Laches bars a suit where a substantial delay by the plaintiff prejudices the defendant. The doctrine of laches bars relief to those who delay the assertion of their claims for an unreasonable time. Laches is founded on the notion that equity should only aid the vigilant. The purpose of laches is to resolve disputes before pertinent evidence becomes lost and defendants rely on their claimed property. There are three affirmative requirements to show laches: (1) a substantial delay by the plaintiff prior to filing suit; (2) awareness that a trademark was being infringed; and (3) reliance by the defendant. In trademark case, reliance is demonstrated where the defendant invests substantial labor and capital to build a name's goodwill. The Association (P) delayed twelve years without informing the LDF (D) that it was challenging the use of the NAACP name. This delay invited reasonable reliance by the LDF (D) and gave it justification to invest resources. Thus, the LDF (D) would be prejudiced by allowing the Association (P) to pursue an infringement action after such a delay. Accordingly, the laches defense to the action was properly brought by the LDF (D). Reversed.

EDITOR'S ANALYSIS: Laches is closely related to estoppel. While laches mainly looks at prejudice that results from a delay, estoppel is concerned with prejudice from misleading action by the plaintiff. The two doctrines begin to merge, and both may be asserted, when the defendant is misled by the plaintiff's silence over time.

NOTES:

BAKER v. F & F INVESTMENT CO.
489 F.2d 829 (7th Cir. 1973).

NATURE OF CASE: Appeal of an interlocutory order denying a motion to dismiss.

FACT SUMMARY: The Federal Housing Administration (D) sought to have a suit by black homeowners (P) in Chicago dismissed on the grounds that the suit had not been filed within Illinois' five-year statute of limitations.

CONCISE RULE OF LAW: A statute of limitations does not bar a suit where there is a continuing violation against the plaintiff.

FACTS: A class of black homeowners (P) in Chicago instituted a suit against the real estate sellers and the Federal Housing Administration (FHA) (D), contending that they were charged excessive and discriminatory prices for their homes. The complaint alleged that the FHA (D) supported the discriminatory market conditions through the administration of home mortgage insurance programs by eliminating the availability of mortgage financing to blacks in Chicago through 1967. The FHA (D) responded that the state's five-year statute of limitations applied from the date that plaintiffs were initially denied mortgage insurance. The court rejected the FHA's (D) motion to dismiss based upon the statute of limitations. The FHA (D) appealed.

ISSUE: Does a statute of limitations bar a suit where there is a continuing violation against the plaintiff?

HOLDING AND DECISION: (Cummings, J.) No. A statute of limitations does not bar a suit where there is a continuing violation against the plaintiff. In situations in which a defendant inflicts a new injury on the plaintiff each day, the statute of limitations does not run from the first day of the violation. Since the defendants can avoid further injury by ceasing their wrongful conduct at any time, the injury continues to accrue. There is no requirement that the parties have a contractual relationship in order to suffer a continuing violation. The FHA (D) could have avoided injuring the black homeowners (P) further if they had offered mortgage insurance at any time during the life of the sales contracts. The refinancing of the homes by the black homeowners (P) may have allowed them to avoid discriminatory finance charges. Therefore, if these claims are proven, the FHA (D) was the source of a continuing violation against the black homeowners (P). Thus, the statute of limitations does not run from the date that they signed their home sales agreements. However, the homeowners (P) are limited to damages which accrued within five years of the suit. Affirmed.

EDITOR'S ANALYSIS: This decision is in accord with the Supreme Court's ruling in Hanvoer v. United Shoe Machinery, 392 U.S. 481 (1968), where the Court held that an antitrust suit for

a discriminatory policy could not be barred simply because it was not challenged forty years prior but that damages had to be limited to the statute period. Three requirements emerge from the cases: (1) the violation must be continuing, (2) the harm must continue, and (3) the continuing violation must cause the harm.

NOTES:

O'BRIEN v. ELI LILLY & CO.
668 F.2d 704 (3d Cir. 1982).

NATURE OF CASE: Appeal from entry of summary judgment denying damages for personal injuries.

FACT SUMMARY: The district court held that O'Brien (P), through the exercise of reasonable diligence, should have discovered her cause of action in 1976, and therefore her case was barred by the statute of limitations.

CONCISE RULE OF LAW: The statute of limitations period for personal injuries begins to run at the time the plaintiff has knowledge of the injury, of the operative cause of the injury, and of the causative relationship between the injury and the operative conduct.

FACTS: O'Brien (P) was told she had cancer in 1971. Shortly before being told this, she read an article in a national newsmagazine describing a high incidence of cancer in the offspring of women who had taken DES, a drug manufactured by Lilly (D) to prevent miscarriages. She asked her doctor if the cancer was related to her mother's use of DES and was told this was probable. She confronted her mother over a period of several years concerning her use of the drug before filing suit in 1979. The trial court granted Lilly's (D) motion for summary judgment, holding the action barred by the statute of limitations. O'Brien (P) appealed, contending the limitations period did not run until she actually discovered the fact that her mother took the drug, and that this involved a question of fact.

ISSUE: Does the statute of limitations begin to run from the time the plaintiff knows of the injury, its cause, and the link between them, or through the exercise of reasonable diligence would have discovered such?

HOLDING AND DECISION: (Aldisert, J.) Yes. The statute of limitations period for personal injuries begins to run at the time the plaintiff has knowledge of the injury, the operative cause of the injury, and of causative relationship, or through the exercise of reasonable diligence such knowledge could be gained. Such diligence would have allowed discovery in 1976, therefore the two-year limitations period barred this action. Affirmed.

CONCURRENCE: (Sloviter, J.) The plaintiff had the same knowledge of her injuries and their causes in 1976 as she did in 1979. Thus, her suit must be barred.

DISSENT: (Higginbotham, J.) The burden of knowledge imposed on the plaintiff exceeds the boundaries of fairness.

EDITOR'S ANALYSIS: This case illustrates the discovery rule applicable to statute of limitations issues. Without such a rule, a case such as the present one creates problems due to the fact there were three possible accrual dates for the cause of action: The wrongful act which occurred in the 1950's when O'Brien's (P) mother was induced to take DES, the injury discovery in 1971, and the causal link discovery in 1976.

NOTES:

KNAYSI v. A.H. ROBINS CO.
679 F.2d 1366 (11th Cir. 1982).

NATURE OF CASE: Appeal from summary judgment denying damages for fraud and products liability.

FACT SUMMARY: Knaysi (P) contended A.H. Robins (D) was equitably estopped from asserting the statute of limitations as a defense to a suit for fraud and products liability.

CONCISE RULE OF LAW: Equitable estoppel sufficient to bar the application of the statute of limitations results from fraudulent concealment of an action which is unknown to a party.

FACTS: Knaysi (P) sued Robins (D), contending the company knew of the dangers inherent in using its Dalkon Shield and intentionally suppressed such information. As a result of using such a device, Knaysi (P) had miscarried twin fetuses. Robins (D) successfully moved for summary judgment on the basis that the fraud claim could not be separated from the products liability action, and such was barred by the statute of limitations. Knaysi (P) appealed, contending Robins (D) was equitably estopped from asserting the statute of limitations as a defense.

ISSUE: Does fraudulent concealment of a cause of action which is unknown to a party give rise to equitable estoppel barring application of the statute of limitations?

HOLDING AND DECISION: (Hill, J.) Yes. Equitable estoppel sufficient to bar the application of the statute of limitations results from fraudulent concealment of an action which is unknown to a party. In this case the medical community and the consuming public relied on Robins' (D) misrepresentations concerning the safety of the product. This misrepresentation creates a question of fact regarding the application of the doctrine of equitable estoppel. Thus summary judgment should not have been granted. Reversed and remanded.

DISSENT: (Tjoflat, J.) The plaintiff failed to meet her burden of establishing justifiable reliance on Robins' (D) alleged misrepresentations. Thus, no question of fact was raised and summary judgement properly entered.

EDITOR'S ANALYSIS: As can be seen by this case, equity can be used to bypass the statute of limitations on legal claims for damages. Equity will not allow the unfairness of fraudulent concealment to preclude an assertion of rights. A minority view goes farther in holding fraudulent concealment equitably estops application of a statute of limitations regardless of the plaintiff's diligence.

CHAPTER 10
REMEDIES AND SEPARATION OF POWERS

QUICK REFERENCE RULES OF LAW

1. **Implied Rights of Action.** A private cause of action for the violation of constitutional rights under color of federal law may be maintained. (Bivens v. Six Unknown Named Agents)

2. **Implied Rights of Action.** The determination whether a federal statute gives rise to a private right of action is based upon the express or implied intent of Congress. (Merrill Lynch, Pierce, Fenner & Smith v. Curran)

3. **Initiating Criminal and Administrative Remedies.** A citizen lacks standing to contest policies of the prosecuting authority when he himself is neither prosecuted nor threatened with prosecution. (Linda R. S. v. Richard D.)

4. **Initiating Criminal and Administrative Remedies.** Plaintiffs only need to show direct exposure to discrimination in order to establish standing to bring suit to force federal agency action. (Women's Equity Action League v. Cavazos)

5. **Suits Against the Government.** A governmental entity may not be liable for failure to provide police protection. (Riss v. City of New York)

6. **Suits against Officers in Their Personal Capacities — Qualified Immunity.** Presidential aides have only a qualified immunity from suit for acts done in their official capacities. (Harlow v. Fitzgerald)

7. **Suits against Officers in Their Personal Capacities — Absolute Immunity.** A judge is immune from suit for any judicial act he performs wherein he has jurisdiction. (Stump v. Sparkman)

BIVENS v. SIX UNKNOWN NAMED AGENTS OF FEDERAL BUREAU OF NARCOTICS
403 U.S. 388 (1971).

NATURE OF CASE: Appeal from dismissal of private action for violation of Fourth Amendment.

FACT SUMMARY: The district court dismissed Bivens'(P) private damages action against six federal agents holding no such cause of action existed under the Fourth Amendment.

CONCISE RULE OF LAW: A private cause of action for the violation of constitutional rights under color of federal law may be maintained.

FACTS: Bivens (P) sued six agents of the Federal Bureau of Narcotics, contending they physically abused and arrested him without a warrant. He contended this action, under color of law, violated his Fourth Amendment rights and entitled him to damages. The district court dismissed the action for failure to state a claim upon which relief could be granted. Bivens (P) appealed, and the court of appeals affirmed. The Supreme Court granted certiorari.

ISSUE: Does a private cause of action exist for violation of constitutional rights under color of law?

HOLDING AND DECISION: (Brennan, J.) Yes. A private cause of action exists for violation of constitutional rights under color of law. Where legal rights have been invaded, courts must fashion remedies to provide relief. The Fourth Amendment grants freedom from unreasonable searches and seizures. If the facts in this case allow a finding of unreasonableness, a damages award would be appropriate. Thus, the lower courts erred in dismissing the action. Reversed.

CONCURRENCE: (Harlan, J.) State remedies for trespass to the person do not preclude a federal cause of action where the tortfeasor acts under color of federal law.

DISSENT: (Burger, J.) This decision violates the separation of powers doctrine by creating a cause of action judicially.

DISSENT: (Black, J.) Congress is the appropriate branch of government to create a private cause of action.

DISSENT: (Blackmun, J.) This is judicial legislation and should be stopped.

EDITOR'S ANALYSIS: This case is the key case creating a private action for violation of constitutional rights. The defense had argued that Bivens (P) should have been required to sue under state tort law. However, this opened the door for the argument that federal agents acting under color of state law have authority exceeding state law.

NOTES:

MERRILL LYNCH, PIERCE, FENNER & SMITH v. CURRAN
456 U.S. 353 (1982).

NATURE OF CASE: Appeals from dismissals of private actions for violations of the Commodities Exchange Act.

FACT SUMMARY: The district courts dismissed four consolidated cases on the basis that there was no private cause of action for violation of the Commodities Exchange Act.

CONCISE RULE OF LAW: The determination whether a federal statute gives rise to a private right of action is based upon the express or implied intent of Congress.

FACTS: In four separate suits consolidated on appeal, the respective trial courts dismissed actions for violation of the Commodities Exchange Act on the basis there existed no private cause of action under that statute. The plaintiffs in all cases appealed, and the Supreme Court granted certiorari.

ISSUE: Is the determination of the existence of a private cause of action based upon the intent of Congress in enacting the statute?

HOLDING AND DECISION: (Stevens, J.) Yes. The determination whether a federal statute gives rise to a private cause of action is based upon the express or implied intent of Congress. In this case the statute was silent. Therefore, Congressional intent must be implied. Prior to amendment, the Commodities Exchange Act was consistently interpreted as including a private cause of action. The amendments and their legislative history in no way changed such an interpretation. Had Congress wished to change the interpretation it would have expressly done so. Its failure to do so implies an intent to continue to recognize the private cause of action. Reversed.

DISSENT: (Powell, J.) The prior cases recognizing a private cause of action violated the separation of powers doctrine and were erroneous.

EDITOR'S ANALYSIS: Another more traditional approach to determining whether a private cause of action exists under a federal law, in the absence of expressed congressional policy, is to determine if the statute is aimed at protecting a particular class. If so, members of that class are generally considered to possess a private cause of action. See Cannon v. University of Chicago, 441 U.S. 677 (1979).

NOTES:

LINDA R.S. v. RICHARD D.
410 U.S. 614 (1973).

NATURE OF CASE: Appeal from denial of injunctive relief.

FACT SUMMARY: Linda (P) sought to force the Texas district attorney to prosecute the father of her child for failure to pay child support.

CONCISE RULE OF LAW: A citizen lacks standing to contest policies of the prosecuting authority when he himself is neither prosecuted nor threatened with prosecution.

FACTS: Linda (P), the mother of an illegitimate child, sought to have the father prosecuted under the criminal statute. The district attorney refused to file charges on the basis he felt illegitimate children were not protected by the statute. Linda (P) sued to enjoin this interpretation of the statute and to force prosecution. The trial court refused to grant the relief, and the Supreme Court granted certiorari.

ISSUE: Does a citizen lack standing to contest policies of the prosecuting authority when he himself is neither prosecuted nor threatened with prosecution?

HOLDING AND DECISION: (Marshall, J.) Yes. A citizen lacks standing to contest policies of the prosecuting authority when he himself is neither prosecuted nor threatened with prosecution. In this case, Linda (P) herself was never threatened with prosecution. Thus, she lacks a recognizable interest in prosecuting the father. She, therefore, has no standing to sue, and the lower court properly dismissed her complaint. Affirmed.

DISSENT: (White, J.) The right to gain relief of a particular type is different from a right to sue. Here the right to sue exists.

DISSENT: (Blackmun, J.) The case should be remanded for clarification of the status of the litigation in light of recent decisional law.

EDITOR'S ANALYSIS: A threshold consideration in any suit is the standing of the parties to sue and be sued. To sue, one must possess an injury which is recognized by the court. Cases which involve only potential injury or injury to another, do not have the right to go forward.

NOTES:

WOMEN'S EQUITY ACTION LEAGUE v. CAVAZOS
879 F.2d 880 (D.C. Cir. 1989).

NATURE OF CASE: Appeal from dismissal of action for injunctive relief directing agency action.

FACT SUMMARY: The Women's Equity Action League (WEAL) (P) sought to force the Department of Health, Education and Welfare (HEW) (D) to process all complaints of racial discrimination barred by Title VI.

CONCISE RULE OF LAW: Plaintiffs only need to show direct exposure to discrimination in order to establish standing to bring suit to force federal agency action.

FACTS: In 1970, suits were initiated against HEW (D) to force the agency to insist on compliance with Title VI. Title VI prohibits discrimination under any federally assisted program on the ground of race. The complaints asserted that HEW (D) was not properly cutting off funding from schools that discriminated. A court ruled that HEW (D) was obliged to affirmatively enforce Title VI by effective means and required HEW (D) to process all complaints of racial discrimination barred by Title VI. In 1976, WEAL (P) intervened in the continuing litigation, seeking enforcement of Title IX of the Education Amendments of 1972. Finally, a consent decree was developed that obligated HEW (D) to follow certain procedures. However, when the Reagan Administration took over in 1981, the consent decree was not followed, and there was a motion to vacate the order. The district court denied the motion to vacate, and HEW (D) appealed. The court of appeals remanded the case for a determination of whether WEAL (P) and the other plaintiffs had standing. The district court held that there was no standing, and WEAL (P) appealed.

ISSUE: Do plaintiffs only need to show direct exposure to discrimination in order to establish standing to bring suit to force federal agency action?

HOLDING AND DECISION: (Ginsburg, J.) Yes. Plaintiffs only need to show direct exposure to discrimination in order to establish standing to bring suit to force federal agency action. In Allen v. Wright, 486 U.S. 737 (1984), the Supreme Court held that there was no standing where the plaintiffs sought to challenge government financial aid to discriminatory schools because the plaintiffs did not seek to attend the schools in question. The stigmatizing injury caused by racial discrimination supports standing only to those persons who are personally denied equal treatment. While Allen excludes bystanders from bringing suit, it preserved court access for persons claiming direct exposure to government-aided facilities which discriminate. To establish standing, plaintiffs do not need to show sure gain but only an enhanced probability of gain. WEAL (P) and the other plaintiffs have not asserted an abstract or generalized grievance but have

asserted a right to be educated in an environment free from discrimination. Thus, they are not bystanders like the plaintiffs in Allen but persons with direct exposure to discrimination. There is at least a possibility that if they are successful in their suit against HEW (D), the exposure to discrimination will cease. Accordingly, WEAL (P) has met the standing requirements. Reversed.

EDITOR'S ANALYSIS: Although courts have ordered HEW (D) to enforce Title VI, previous courts had refused to order federal prosecutors to prosecute criminal and civil offenses. These courts had ruled that the decision to prosecute must be left to prosecutorial discretion. See Adams v. Richardson, 480 F.2d 1159 (D.C. Cir. 1973). The WEAL court, however, attempted to distinguish these cases by citing the directive of Title VI specifically requiring HEW's (D) enforcement.

NOTES:

RISS v. CITY OF NEW YORK

N.Y. Ct. App., 22 N.Y. 2d 579, 240 N.E.2d 860 (1968).

NATURE OF CASE: Appeal of dismissal of action for failure to provide police protection.

FACT SUMMARY: Riss (P), harassed for months by a former suitor, had repeatedly asked for police protection prior to an assault.

CONCISE RULE OF LAW: A governmental entity may not be liable for failure to provide police protection.

FACTS: For six months Linda Riss (P) had been threatened by a former suitor. Riss (P) continually asked for police protection but was largely ignored. Riss (P) became engaged. The former suitor then hired a thug, who threw caustic lye in her face, partially blinding and also scarring her. Riss (P) brought an action against the City of New York (D) for failure to provide police protection. The trial court dismissed the complaint, and the appellate division affirmed.

ISSUE: May a governmental entity be liable for failure to provide police protection?

HOLDING AND DECISION: (Breitel, J.) No. A governmental entity may not be liable for failure to provide police protection. It is one thing to hold such an entity liable for ordinary torts. It is quite another to expose the entity to the type of liability sought here. To do this would amount to allowing courts and citizens to decide how such entities will allocate resources. Such a serious restructuring of governmental decision-making power should only come from the legislature, not the courts. Affirmed.

DISSENT: (Keating, J.) The City (D) failed in its duty to protect Riss (P). The costs of allowing such liability would not be as great as the court contends. Finally, it is proper for courts to review administrative decisions.

EDITOR'S ANALYSIS: The concept of sovereign immunity has always been controversial. Once the universal rule, it has now been fully or partially abrogated in most jurisdictions. Even where it no longer exists, there are often procedural obstacles a plaintiff must hurdle to sue a governmental entity.

NOTES:

HARLOW v. FITZGERALD
457 U.S. 800 (1987).

NATURE OF CASE: Appeal of denial of summary judgment in action for conspiracy.

FACT SUMMARY: Fitzgerald (P) brought an action against former Nixon White House aides for conspiring to oust him from his job.

CONCISE RULE OF LAW: Presidential aides have only a qualified immunity from suit for acts done in their official capacities.

FACTS: Fitzgerald (P), a management analyst in the Air Force, "blew the whistle" regarding certain questionable weapons procurement practices. His job was subsequently taken out from under him, and he eventually brought suit against Harlow (D), a White House aide, and others for conspiring to retaliate against him. Fitzgerald (P) alleged that Harlow (D) conspired with the other defendants to achieve a reduction in force in his department merely to get him out of the civil service. Harlow (D) moved for summary judgment based on a contention of absolute immunity. This was denied, and the court of appeals affirmed.

ISSUE: Do presidential aides have only a qualified immunity for acts done in their official capacities?

HOLDING AND DECISION: (Powell, J.) Yes. Presidential aides have only a qualified immunity for acts done in their official capacities. Immunity is based on the notion that an official must be able to perform his tasks without worrying about potential legal liability. However, immunity extracts a social price, and therefore absolute immunity will be granted only when necessary. By and large, presidential aides can be given such immunity only when they are acting as direct alter egos of the President, something not often occurring. Other than at those times, the privilege White House aides should enjoy is one of "good faith." If the official was reasonably unaware that his conduct constituted a violation of the Constitution or statutes, he will be granted immunity. This action must be remanded to allow Harlow (P) to plead facts which will defeat this sort of privilege.

CONCURRENCE: (Brennan, J.) An official actually knowing he is violating the law should not be immune.

CONCURRENCE: (Brennan, J.) To the extent this opinion approves Nixon v. Fitzgerald, we do not concur in the opinion.

CONCURRENCE: (Rehnquist, J.) The rule enunciated here is in accord with the law, but the law should be reexamined.

DISSENT: (Burger, C.J.) Senior White House aides should have absolute immunity deriving from the President.

EDITOR'S ANALYSIS: Both the Court's opinion and Chief Justice Burger's dissent discuss "derivative immunity." As the name indicates, it is immunity deriving from another source, here the President. This sort of immunity is recognized in legislative aides. However, the circumstances under which this immunity applies are narrow.

NOTES:

STUMP v. SPARKMAN
435 U.S. 349 (1978).

NATURE OF CASE: Appeal of reversal of dismissal of civil rights action.

FACT SUMMARY: Sparkman (P) instituted an action against a judge who had approved a sterilization procedure on her during her minority.

CONCISE RULE OF LAW: A judge is immune from suit for any judicial act he performs wherein he has jurisdiction.

FACTS: Sparkman's (P) mother presented to state court judge Stump (D) a petition to have Sparkman (P) sterilized, stating that Sparkman (P), a minor, was retarded and that her sexual behavior could not be monitored. The judge approved that petition, and the procedure was performed, Sparkman (P) believing the surgery to be an appendectomy. Sparkman (P) became aware of the facts several years later and brought an action against Stump (D) for civil rights violations, and various state claims against her mother and doctors. The district court held that Stump (D) was protected by judicial immunity, and dismissed the action. The court of appeals reversed. Stump (D) appealed.

ISSUE: Is a judge immune from suit for any judicial act he performs wherein he has jurisdiction?

HOLDING AND DECISION: (White, J.) Yes. A judge is immune from suit for any judicial act he performs wherein he has jurisdiction. It has long been established that the orderly administration of law requires that judicial officers be allowed to make decisions unhampered by fears of private liability. Whenever a judge acts within his subject matter jurisdiction, he may not be so liable, even if he acts negligently, corruptly, or exceeds his jurisdiction. Therefore, the only way Sparkman (P) could recover here is if Stump (D) did not have subject matter jurisdiction. Stump (D) was a judge of general jurisdiction and, absent an express limitation on his power in this area, which did not exist, had jurisdiction. Therefore, the argument that Stump (D) violated due process is irrelevant. Reversed.

DISSENT: (Stewart, J.) Stump's (D) act was not judicial in nature; approving a minor's sterilization is not a normal judicial act.

DISSENT: (Powell, J.) Stump's (D) act was nonjudicial, and to hold it judicial forecloses any relief to Sparkman (D).

EDITOR'S ANALYSIS: The degree to which governmental officers are immune from suit varies from office to office. For instance, legislators are immune from defamation for anything they say during a legislative proceeding. Congressional aides have a lesser immunity. Judges appear to have the most, this being the "absolute immunity" of which the Court speaks.

NOTES:

101

CHAUFFEURS LOCAL NO. 391 v. TERRY
494 U.S. 558 (1990).

NATURE OF CASE: Interlocutory appeal of an order granting a jury trial in an action for breach of collective bargaining action.

FACT SUMMARY: Terry (P) and other truck drivers (P) sought a jury trial in an action against Chauffeurs Local No. 391 (D), their union, for breach of its duty to fairly represent them in a grievance proceeding.

CONCISE RULE OF LAW: The right to a jury trial under the Seventh Amendment depends on the nature of the issue to be tried and the remedy sought, rather than the character of the overall action.

FACTS: Terry (P) and a group of other truck drivers were transferred to work in Winston-Salem, North Carolina. An argument ensued between these new drivers (P) and other drivers in Winston-Salem over seniority rules. Both groups of drivers were part of Chauffeurs Local No. 319 (D). In a grievance proceeding, the Union (D) took the side of the original drivers, and the Terry (P) group was subsequently laid off. Terry (P) filed suit against the Union (D) for breach of the collective bargaining agreement. Terry (P) asserted that Chauffeurs Local (D) had breached its duty to fairly represent them and sought a jury trial. The Union (D) responded that the suit was analogous to an action by a trust beneficiary, which was an action in equity, so Terry (P) was not entitled to a jury trial. The district court ruled for Terry (P), and Chauffeurs Local (D) appealed.

ISSUE: Does the right to a jury trial under the Seventh Amendment depend on the nature of the issue to be tried and the remedy that is sought?

HOLDING AND DECISION: (Marshall, J.) Yes. The right to a jury trial under the Seventh Amendment depends on the nature of the issue to be tried and the remedy sought, rather than the character of the overall action. The Seventh Amendment provides for a right to a jury trial in a "suit at common law." Thus, in order to determine whether a plaintiff has a right to a trial by jury the court must examine the nature of the issues involved and the remedy sought. If the nature of the issue is similar to an action that was tried in a court of law before the merger of the courts of law and equity, the parties will be entitled to a jury trial. Also, the court must determine whether the remedy sought is legal or equitable in nature. A suit for breach of the duty of fair representation for union members resembles an action by a trust beneficiary against a trustee. This type of action was equitable in nature. However, the breach of collective bargaining agreement resembles a breach of contract action. Thus, the nature of the whole issue is both legal and equitable. However, the remedy sought by Terry (P) is monetary damages. This remedy is legal in nature. Accordingly, Terry (P) has a right to a jury trial because the nature of the issue is both legal and equitable but the remedy sought is legal. Affirmed.

CONCURRENCE: (Brennan, J.) The inquiry required by the majority is too difficult for trial courts. The Seventh Amendment question should be decided on the basis of the relief sought.

DISSENT: (Kennedy, J.) Taken as a whole, Terry's (P) action most resembles a suit by a trust beneficiary which would have been heard by a court of equity at the time of the Seventh Amendment. Thus, there should be no right to trial by jury.

EDITOR'S ANALYSIS: The leading case on the Seventh Amendment is Beacon Theatres v. Westover, 359 U.S. 500 (1959). In that case, the Court decided that the merger of law and equity had changed the scope of the Seventh Amendment since equitable remedies were now available for legal actions. Beacon is still good law today.

NOTES:

CHAPTER 11
FLUID CLASS REMEDIES

QUICK REFERENCE RULES OF LAW

1. **Fluid Class Remedies.** Courts in attempting to certify class actions pursuant to Rule 23 must still adhere to the procedural safeguards stated in the rule, even if such adherence requires dismissal of the action as a class action. (Eisen v. Carlisle & Jacquelin)

EISEN v. CARLISLE & JACQUELIN
479 F.2d 1005 (2nd Cir. 1973).

NATURE OF CASE: Appeal from decision allowing class action antitrust suit to proceed.

FACT SUMMARY: Carlisle and Jacquelin (C & J) (D) appealed from a district court decision in an antitrust case allowing the action to proceed as a class action.

CONCISE RULE OF LAW: Courts in attempting to certify class actions pursuant to Rule 23 must still adhere to the procedural safeguards stated in the rule, even if such adherence requires dismissal of the action as a class action.

FACTS: Eisen (P) brought an action against C & J (D), who handled odd lot transactions on the New York Stock Exchange. It was an antitrust action contending that C & J (D), who handled 99% of the odd lot transactions, fixed commissions on those transactions at an excessive level. Class certification was initially designed. The court of appeals decided that decision was an appealable final judgment because the decision rendered the suit economically impossible to proceed. Upon remand, the district court concluded that the action could proceed as a class action, the class being all persons who bought or sold odd lot transactions during the time period alleged in the suit. Evidence indicated there were 6,000,000 members in the class of which 2,250,000 were easily identifiable. The district court designed a series of notices to be provided in this case, held a brief minihearing on the merits of the case, and pursuant to that hearing it ordered C & J (D) to pay 90% of the costs of notifying the members of the class. From the decision to allow the case to proceed as a class action and requiring the C & J (D) to pay a portion of the costs of the notice, C & J (D) appealed.

ISSUE: Can the courts fashion equitable remedies in an effort to make actions economically unfeasible by individual plaintiffs actionable as class actions without complying with the procedural safeguards that exist in Rule 23?

HOLDING AND DECISION: (Medina, J.) No. Courts in attempting to certify class actions pursuant to Rule 23 must still adhere to the procedural safeguards as stated in the rule, even if such adherence will result in the dismissal of the action as a class action. Rule 23 unambiguously provides that the plaintiff pay the costs of giving notice to the easily identifiable members of the class. Nor does Rule 23 provide for any makeshift, preliminary minihearing on the merits of the action prior to the giving of the required notice as provided in the rule. The economics of this particular action are quite clear in providing that the damages recoverable by each individual plaintiff are so small that individual actions as a practical matter could not be maintained. The court has recognized that this case is unmanageable as a class action, but the attempt to institute a form of "fluid class recovery" in this case falls short. Cases relied on by counsel for Eisen (P) are clearly distinguishable. Even though the court recognizes that adherence to the procedural safeguards in Rule 23 makes actions like the present case impossible to bring, the remedy is one for the legislature to fashion and should not circumvent the procedures designed to prevent oppression and in the long run designed to benefit all litigants. Reversed; dismissed as a class action; rehearing en banc denied.

DISSENT: (Oakes, J.) (From denial of rehearing en banc.) The decision denying rehearing of the issues presented in this case allows monopolies and conglomerates to violate the antitrust laws with relative impunity, free from any realistic threat of private consumer civil proceedings. Assuming vigorous representation of the class' interests by Eisen (P) in this case, which has not been questioned, the notice contemplated by the court, via publication, is constitutionally sufficient.

EDITOR'S ANALYSIS: This case was unanimously affirmed by the Supreme Court, 417 U.S. 156 (1974). Although it is a possibility that such wrongdoing may go unaddressed, from a purely economic standpoint, it may be a waste of resources to attempt to recover such small sums absent an administratively efficient remedy, which is at present nonexistent.

NOTES:

NOTES

TOTAL *the* STUDY *Team*

casenote™ LEGAL BRIEFS
America's best selling legal briefs

Features: casenote® CASE CAPSULES
States essence of the case at a glance

▶ **COMPLETE BRIEFS** *The most comprehensive briefs; concurrences and dissents are never omitted; judge's names are included; no sketchy summaries; editor's analysis discusses case relevance.*

▶ **ALL MAJOR CASES BRIEFED** *All cases appearing in bold face titles in casebook are briefed in your CASENOTES.*

▶ **TRUE-TO-CASE EXCERPTS** *Cases are briefed according to the way in which they are edited by your casebook editor.*

▶ **FREE SUPPLEMENT UPDATE SERVICE** *CASENOTES are always made complete whenever a casebook supplement is issued.*

▶ **OVER 170 TITLES**

and

LAW OUTLINES from CASENOTE™

the Ultimate Outline

▶ *WRITTEN BY NATIONALLY RECOGNIZED AUTHORITIES IN THEIR FIELD.*

▶ *FEATURING A FLEXIBLE, SUBJECT-ORIENTED APPROACH.*

▶ *CONTAINS: TABLE OF CONTENTS; CAPSULE OUTLINE; FULL OUTLINE; EXAM PREPARATION; GLOSSARY; TABLE OF CASES; TABLE OF AUTHORITIES; CASEBOOK CROSS-REFERENCE CHART; INDEX.*

▶ *THE TOTAL LAW SUMMARY UTILIZING THE MOST COMPREHENSIVE STUDY APPROACH IN THE MOST EFFECTIVE, EASY-TO-READ FORMAT.*

REF #	SUBJECT	AUTHORS	RETAIL PRICE
#5260	ADMINISTRATIVE LAW by **Charles H. Koch, Jr.,** Dudley W. Woodbridge Professor of Law, College of William and Mary. **Sidney A. Shapiro,** John M. Rounds Professor of Law, University of Kansas. (1996) w/'98 supp.)		(effective 7/1/98) $20.95
#5040	CIVIL PROCEDURE by **John B. Oakley,** Professor of Law, University of California, Davis. **Rex R. Perschbacher,** Professor of Law & Associate Dean, Academic Affairs, University of California, Davis. (1996)		$21.95
	COMMERCIAL LAW (see 5700 SALES ● 5710 SECURED TRANS. ● 5720 NEG. INSTRUMENTS & PMT. SYST.)		
#5070	CONFLICT OF LAWS by **Luther L. McDougal, III,** W.R. Irby Professor of Law, Tulane University. **Robert L. Felix,** James P. Mozingo, III Professor of Law, University of South Carolina. (1996)		$20.95
#5080	CONSTITUTIONAL LAW by **Gary Goodpaster,** Prof. of Law, Univ. of Calif., Davis. (1997 w/'98 supp.)		$23.95
#5010	CONTRACTS by **Daniel Wm. Fessler,** Professor of Law, University of California, Davis. (1996)		$20.95
#5050	CORPORATIONS by **Lewis D. Solomon,** Arthur Selwin Miller Research Prof. of Law, George Washington Univ. AND ALTERNATIVE BUSINESS VEHICLES **Daniel Wm. Fessler,** Professor of Law, University of California, Davis. **Arthur E. Wilmarth, Jr.,** Associate Professor of Law, George Washington University. (1997)		$23.95
#5020	CRIMINAL LAW by **Joshua Dressler,** Professor of Law, McGeorge School of Law. (1996)		$20.95
#5200	CRIMINAL PROCEDURE by **Joshua Dressler,** Prof. of Law, McGeorge School of Law. (1997)		$19.95
#5800	ESTATE & GIFT TAX by **Joseph M. Dodge,** W.H. Francis Professor of Law, University of INCLUDING THE FEDERAL GENERATION-SKIPPING TAX Texas at Austin. (w/ supp. due Fall 1998)		$20.95
#5060	EVIDENCE by **Kenneth Graham, Jr.,** Professor of Law, University of California, Los Angeles. (1996)		$22.95
#5400	FEDERAL COURTS by **Howard P. Fink,** Isadore and Ida Topper Prof. of Law, Ohio State. Univ. **Linda S. Mullenix,** Bernard J. Ward Centennial Prof. of Law, Univ. of Texas. (1997)		$21.95
#5210	FEDERAL INCOME TAXATION by **Joseph M. Dodge,** W.H. Francis Professor of Law, University of Texas at Austin (1998).		$21.95
#5300	LEGAL RESEARCH by **Nancy L. Schultz,** Associate Professor of Law, Chapman University. **Louis J. Sirico, Jr.,** Professor of Law, Villanova University School of Law. (1996)		$20.95
#5720	NEGOTIABLE INSTRUMENTS & PMT. SYST. by **Donald B. King,** Prof. of Law, St. Louis Univ. **Peter Winship,** James Cleo Thompson Sr. Trustee Professor, Southern Methodist University. (1995)		$21.95
#5030	PROPERTY by **Sheldon F. Kurtz,** Percy Bordwell Professor of Law, University of Iowa, and **Patricia Cain,** Professor of Law, University of Iowa (1997).		$21.95
#5700	SALES by **Robert E. Scott,** Dean and Lewis F. Powell, Jr. Professor of Law, University of Virginia. **Donald B. King,** Professor of Law, St. Louis University. (1992)		$20.95
#5710	SECURED TRANSACTIONS by **Donald B. King,** Professor of Law, St. Louis Univ. (1995 w/'96 supp.)		$19.95
#5000	TORTS by **George C. Christie,** James B. Duke Professor of Law, Duke University. **Jerry J. Phillips,** W.P. Toms Professor of Law & Chair, Committee on Admissions, University of Tennessee. (1996 w/'98 supp.)		$21.95
#5220	WILLS, TRUSTS & ESTATES by **William M. McGovern,** Professor of Law, University of California, Los Angeles. (1996)		$21.95

rev. 1/1/98